WOUNDS CAUSED BY GOSSIP

ATTITUDES AND CONFLICTS IN THE WORKPLACE

How to deal with difficult people
and situations on the job

O.C. ISOM II

authorHOUSE®

AuthorHouse™ LLC
1663 Liberty Drive
Bloomington, IN 47403
www.authorhouse.com
Phone: 1-800-839-8640

Published by AuthorHouse   07/02/2014

ISBN: 978-1-4969-0089-0 (sc)
ISBN: 978-1-4969-0088-3 (hc)
ISBN: 978-1-4969-0087-6 (e)

Library of Congress Control Number: 2014910824

Presented To:

_____

From:

_____

Date:

_____

DEDICATION

This book is dedicated to all employers and employees who are or have been facing gossip and/or conflicts that have caused scars and wounds in the workplace. It is our desire to create a healthy environment among employees within the workplace by providing them with the insight and skills in order to be effective in workplace.

*"Individual
commitment to a
group effort - that
is what makes
a team work, a
company work,
a society work, a
civilization work."*

— VINCENT LOMBARDI

TABLE OF CONTENTS

ACKOWLEDGEMENTS

First of all, I want to give thanks, glory, and honor to God for giving me this desire and enabling me to help others gain their freedom and knowledge in a workplace.

Thank you to all the co-workers, leaders, and CEO's around the world who have taken the time to understand and show hard work and patience in order to better understand their challenging employees, and the various attitudes that exist in the workplace today.

Special thanks to all the employees, leaders, and CEOs we interviewed during the formation of this book. The vital information provided helped me to better understand what exactly is going on within the workplace that may cause preventable hurt, pain, emotional wounds and stagnation.

Special thanks goes out to all my readers who will read this book and begin the journey toward a commitment, dedication and a positive attitude in workplace.

Finally, I thank God for my beautiful family, co-workers and all the members of Word Up Apostolic Ministries, who encouraged and convinced me of the need to write a book on gossip and conflict in the workplace. So, from my heart, the words "Thank you" are not enough, so I'll just say, "To God be the Glory".

INTRODUCTION

A person's attitude in the workplace has a direct bearing on one's life. It reveals what one is feeling on the inside, and sometimes it will reflect on things that will cause an unintended reaction toward one's co-workers. Attitudes are very important in the workplace because they govern a person's life, can alter one's character, and determine how one may handle different situations, when working amongst one's co-workers. An attitude is a state of mind or feeling; these feelings can be positive or negative, based on observation, judgment, and/or certain behavior. Many employees have developed strong negative attitudes toward the workforce which in turn have brought about chaos and havoc amongst those with whom they work.

We have looked at gossip and conflict through interviewing several employees and employers. After gathering the information from them, we have come up with a sound conclusion that there are major problems in the workplace that need to be addressed and exposed. The main reason for most disorder, division, emotional wounds and hatred amongst employees, which causes their emotions to change, is gossip. In turn, that causes the workload to seize. When workers cannot get along with each other, it may cause the production at work to either move slowly or come to a halt. When unresolved issues are ignored in the workplace, conflicts are obvious, such as quality problems that may arise when employees act on their anger and frustration, instead of acting with cooperation and a positive attitude.

It can be hard to come to work every day, especially when you know you have to deal with difficult people. There are many strategies and information in this book that co-workers can develop and learn how to have a smoother relationship in workplace. This book provides the vital information needed by any organization to develop wellness programs and enhance healthy life styles among associates. By taking a proactive approach to improving your relationship, you may be able to clear up misunderstandings and smooth the way to a better work environment.

That why it is so important for leaders and co-workers to focus on building trust, pride and camaraderie every step of the way to build a strong team in workplace. Every associate in the workplace must realize that your team environment begins with you.

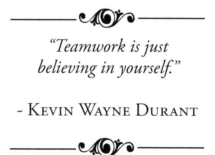

"Teamwork is just believing in yourself."

- Kevin Wayne Durant

Having a *workforce continuity plan* is critical in developing a relationship among employers and employees that will cause the team and organization to grow in a positive direction. So every employer and employee must realize people, who are successful in any workplace, did not get there by themselves. You can interpret that lots of different ways, but what I'm saying is, **it takes a team in order to succeed.** This book will equip and train you on how to deal with difficult people and situations in the workplace.

Difficult people will show up for work with all kinds of attitudes, and they have an uncanny way of saying things that just dampen your day. They can always be counted on to bring out the worst in you, to be obtuse and disagreeable, to make easy things seem impossible, to put a negative spin on the things you do, to speak ill of you, or to ignite an inextinguishable fire in your life that will bring about conflicts. As much as we wish that difficult people would just go away, this will never happen. Just be proactive when someone negative comes to you; treat them with respect and you can never go wrong by displaying Christ-like love and a teamwork attitude.

"A team environment is all about A-Team. When one messes up, we all mess up because we all are a team working toward a common goal. A team is created by a group of individuals who have a purpose for working together, a positive attitude, making the workload manageable, and who are not afraid of change."

–O.C. Isom

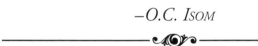

We as Co-workers can't afford to let any bad attitudes to get in the way that will affect your team environment. Working on a job with employees who have a bad attitude is not an easy task as you see your co-workers going around whispering and speaking evil about you. That is why when you, as an employee, go on your job; you must keep one thing in mind: **You are not there to assassinate other peoples' characters.** It is my heartfelt goal that this book will give you some insight and moral guidance that will lead you to go on your job with full motivation and keep one main purpose in mind I here as a servant to the Lord and **to work as a team and to serve my customers.**

"The greatest discovery of my generation is that human beings can alter their lives by altering their attitude of mind."

— WILLIAM JAMES, PSYCHOLOGIST

CHAPTER 1

WE MUST COMMUNICATE

We live in a world made up of diverse people that have different backgrounds, nationalities, lifestyles, and capabilities. While working together and socializing in our personal and professional lives, we need each other for security, comfort, friendship, and love. However, in our working environment, we need each other in order to achieve our goals, aspirations, and objectives. None of these goals can be achieved without communication. Because communication is the foundation of any kind of relationships, this is how our culture is shaped.

Communication is a skill. Communication is the glue that holds a society together. The ability to communicate enables people to form and maintain personal relationships, and the quality of such relationships will always depends on the caliber of communication between the parties. Through communication, we make known our needs, our wants, our ideas, our desires, our aspirations, and our feelings. The better we are at communication, the more effective we are at achieving our hopes and dreams. We must establish ourselves as effective communicators. We must, first, establish credibility. In the business arena, this involves displaying knowledge of the subject, audience and the context in which the message is delivered. You must also know your audience (individuals or groups to which you are delivering your message). Failure to understand who you are communicating to will result in delivering messages that may be misunderstood. As in any relationship, communication is the key to a strong successful relationship. Here are some ways to keep the communication and the relationship flowing:

- Communication through speech, writing, email, telephone or videoconferencing
- Written, oral, and nonverbal communications are affected by the sender's tone
- Messages are conveyed through channels of expression, which can be nonverbal or face-to-face interaction

These are some of the different methods of communication that are commonly used within many workplaces today to communicate information. This can be the relationship between business companies and customers, or, equally as important, the internal relationships among different employees within the company. Communication can be improved in virtually every workplace, no matter the industry or size. After all, it is the only way for information to effectively spread throughout the business so that everybody can be informed to the degree that they require to properly achieve their goals. Ineffective or poor communication leads to distortion of information, or failure to understand the message, which in turn proves to be frustrating for employees, and thus becomes a source of a conflict. A manager's inability to clearly express their thoughts, ideas, and demands leads to employees' inability to perform work well, according to the company's demands. That is why more than often poor communication can lead to:

- Misunderstandings
- Lack of information

- Decrease in employees' performance
- Decrease in company's turnover, as a result
- Disagreements
- Behavior and attitudes

Effective communication in the workplace provides employees with a clear understanding of what is demanded from them, with knowledge of what to do and what to expect. When employees have a lack of communication in the workplace, it will wreck your company's culture. Be proactive and interactive, and encourage an environment of open, healthy communication so that your employees can achieve their true potential, and your business can be a truly successful one. For any organization desires their company to grow and expand, communication is the foundation that will create effective performance of the staff, and, consequently, increase customer loyalty and profit for growth.

"Communication is the LIFELINE of any relationship. When you stop communicating, you start losing your valuable relationship."

- UNKNOWN

COMMUNICATION IS A TWO-WAY STREET

Communication is a two-way process. Although, communication is successful only when the receiver understands the message intended by the sender. Time and again, many corporations have spent phenomenal sums of time and money to uncover corporate flaws and improve production in the workplace.

When there is a two-way communication process, two people or groups are able to communicate with each other in an interchangeable way. What this means is that one person or group will express an ideal, which is received and comprehend by the other person or group. When the receiver processes what has been said, and returns with a message that is then received by the initial speaker, allowing both sides to interact in the process to communicate and understand each side.

"Coming together is a beginning. Keeping together is process. Working together is success."

— HENRY FORD

Employers and employees — you need one another. Everyone has unique abilities, hence, the need to value each and every one's contribution. That's why it is important that no one in the workplace tries to do the work alone. It has been said that a reputation is what people think we are, but character is what we really are. Character, like the grain of sand in the oyster that produces the beautiful pearl, is developed after employees spend time with one another, hence, forming a rapport that causes them to birth a character of pearls among each other.

When every associate in the workplace begins to demonstrate two-way communication or a public relations process in which employees and other groups share different ideals, those in the workplace must work together and learn together to build strong a strong organization, team and communities.

Communicating effectively in the workplace effectively is very essential for smooth and efficient functioning of an organization. The manager should have proper communication skills with his subordinates, or else it will lead to absenteeism among workers, lower productivity, and the development of a grapevine network in an organization.

There should be a two-way communication in an organization among co-workers, as well. A manager should have a personal contact with his subordinates. He should clearly communicate goals and policies of the organization to his subordinates and should get feedback on these goals and policies. Feedback plays a very important role in the communication process in the workplace. It enables us to evaluate the effectiveness of our message, giving the subordinates a chance to provide open communication to create an environment that encourages feedback among co-workers.

PERCEPTION IMPACT COMMUNICATION

Perception is the process through which people select, organize, and interpret sensory input to give meaning and order to the world around them. Perception is inherently subjective and influenced by people's personalities, values, attitudes, moods, experience, and knowledge. When senders and receivers communicate with each other, they are doing so based on their own subjective perceptions. Everybody perceives things differently. That does not mean that one person is right and the other wrong. It does mean that communication between individuals, who have different perspectives, requires more understanding, negation, persuasion, and tolerance of those differences. Perception plays a central role in communication and affects both transmission and feedback of information.

"Communication is depositing a part of yourself in another person."

– ANONYMOUS

Furthermore, the way in which people communicate at the place of work can actually be the cause of poor communication in the workplace. Even when the person with the information believes that she/he has shared this information with all of the right people, this may not exactly be true. After all, some people are better at communicating than others, and when someone, who struggles to express themselves, is the source of the necessary information, this causes a problem.

Ideally, people should communicate clearly, at a comfortable pace, with a practical vocabulary and in an engaging tone. They need to get to the point before the listener can lose interest or miss the point altogether. Unfortunately, this isn't always the case. Often, people speak too quickly or slowly for us to properly absorb what is being said. They may be too loud or too quiet, use words that we don't understand, or use words that are so juvenile that they don't express the proper degrees and details required for the statement. They may speak in a shrill or singsong tone that is distracting, causing us to lose the information before it enters our minds.

Perception may also be influenced by moods as if an individual is having a very hard day or going through personal problems than any even slightly negative aspects of communication will provoke a reaction or likely result in the other person being ignored. Perception is reality. Perception, when it comes to communication in the workplace, determines how one will communicate and how they will receive information from another person. Once employees develop a positive perception in the workplace, customer service efforts will receive a positive response. Your perception of others is the product of how you view yourself. You will remember things better if you relate to self and if you tend to ignore that which contrasts with the way you view yourself.

"Many relationship problems are rooted in a communication break-down. These can be as simple as not really hearing what the other person is saying, because we get caught up in our own fixed perspectives."

-SUMESH NAIR

IMPORTANCE OF COMMUNICATION

Communication is defined primarily as an exchange of ideas. Through every means available to employees, they should always seek to convey their thoughts, desires, plans, and needs to one another. Employees should always feel free to communicate with one another, because this is vital to complete communication. We, as employers and employees, must communicate with one another. It is important that every time when we come to work, we must have a free flow of information between and among employees and employers to improve production.

Many employees and employers don't realize the gap created when information is not properly communicated or disseminated among the intended players. One of the major challenges at the place of work is when employees fail to communicate with each other. Many employees feel they can operate alone. Loneliness is always caused by certain issues in the workplace. There are people in the workplace, who are self-centered and have robbed the company a great deal of a healthy relationship among the co-workers. There are employers and employees, who think since they have been on a job for a certain number of years, they feel they know everything, hence they refuse to share information with other people. So, in reality, associates must realize that there is a right way and a wrong way to deal with people who think they know everything. Avoiding them will not help them to see that they don't know everything. You can, however, take the time to show them that they don't. When those in workplace see you are a very positive and professional person and you know what you are talking about, they will be less inclined to challenge you.

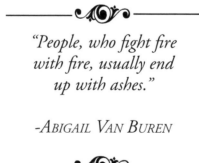

*"People, who fight fire
with fire, usually end
up with ashes."*

-*ABIGAIL VAN BUREN*

POOR COMMUNICATION SKILLS IN THE WORKPLACE

Morale problems have infiltrated the workplace of today, and this issue is steadily eating away the employee relationships, which are vital for an organization's smooth running. As a result, job turnover is high, morale is low, and job security is practically nonexistent. One major corporation paid for professional advice to come in to every workplace and do a study of their employees and managers. They submitted a final report, and one key flaw often found, which contributed significantly to the problems, was poor communication or the lack of communication.

"Improving poor communication skills can make a huge difference in the way that you relate to others."

-UNKNOWN

Poor communication in the workplace can lead to poor relations between employees and an unfriendly work atmosphere, in general, that renders workers inefficient and ineffective. This leads workers to reciprocate their feelings towards their customers. Poor communication in the workplace can damage one's chances to further their self in that organization. Poor communication can cause an organization to relay the wrong message to potential clients, which can damage the company. Proper communication promotes trust. When individuals convey words, gestures or facial expressions ineffectively strain or destroy relationships at work and home. Other problems are omitting details, forgetting to relay important information and failing to listen actively.

Many co-workers in workplaces refuse to communicate with one another either because they can't stand one another or they have some issues with someone. Co-workers must overcome every issue of poor communication in the workplace; it may not always be easy. When resolving the situation in your workplace, remember to give it time, and motivate the employees properly.

However, communication is a process by which information is exchanged between individuals through a common language or system of symbols, signs, or behaviors. Communication requires more than one person. For communication to happen successfully, both parties have to participate, perhaps reciprocally. One is actively communicating; the other is actively listening.

When we deal with poor communication, it comes in many different forms. Here are some examples of poor ineffective communication in the workplace:

- Venting
- Blaming
- Threats
- Yelling
- Silent-treatment or never talking
- Refuse to make the information plain
- Rehearsing the past

These are childish attitudes that many managers and co-workers display every day on the job that bring about hurt feelings because of poor communication. There is a way to talk to your co-workers without using degrading words just because you having a bad day, family issues or because you have the authority or many years of services on the job. People are human, and they do have feelings. Many people's emotions have been hurt, which have caused emotional wounds and bitterness in their life toward those in the workplace, who have authority, because of their poor attitudes skills.

"You catch more flies with honey than you do with vinegar." This phrase would indicate that *you make more friends by being nice than by being rude.* Usually, many people in the workplace refuse to live by this phrase. Sometimes, people take a person being nice as a doormat. They assume you're weak. Or, if you aren't in people's faces all the time, they ignore you or don't think you're worth listening to. We, as a team, should treat people how we would like them to treat us. Remember the "Golden Rule".

Therefore all things whatsoever ye would that men should do to you, do ye even so to them; for this is the law and the prophets (Matthew 7:12).

In the workplace, "interpersonal relations" is not usually thought of as a Bible topic, but advice about dealing with other people. Whether dealing with our parents, children, spouses, friends, co-workers, church members or even our enemies, the Bible's advice is spiritually sound and effective for promoting peace and harmony. This spiritual attitude will eradicate judging, criticizing, condemning and being self –righteousness. The Golden Rule, spoken by Jesus, is possibly the best-known quote from the Bible and is the standard Jesus set for dealing with other people. If we wish to be loved, we must give love. If we wish to be respected, we must respect all persons, even those we dislike. If we wish to be forgiven, we must also forgive. If we wish others to speak kindly of us, we must speak kindly of them and avoid gossip. If we want happy marriages, we must be faithful, forgiving and kind to our spouses. If we wish to be fulfilled in our lives, we must share generously with others.

Speaking nicely to other people is about using your empathy to be considerate of others. It is about saying things clearly so that you are understood well. Speaking nicely also involves thinking before you speak, in order to put aside any of your own hostilities, annoyances and gripes that can cause tension or upset when holding a conversation or discussion. Speaking kind words to one another will bring about a relationship in the workplace.

Let your speech be always with grace, seasoned with salt, that ye may know how ye ought to answer every man (Colossians 4:6).

Poor communication can be daunting. There are many remedies that can help alleviate the many problems of poor communication that exist in the workplace among co-workers. Educational and training is essential and must be done continuously in order for employees to cease and improve upon poor communication. Lack of communication in the workplace can occur on a large scale, such as between management and employees, as well as on a smaller scale between individual employees. Failure to communicate effectively often leads to conflict, which can harm an organization.

Poor communication can create conflict in a number of ways. Studies show that a lack of communication is the number one reason couples get divorced. In the workplace, when it comes to communication, more employees are disconnected than ever. Miscommunication and refusal to communicate can contribute to problems and conflicts in the workplace.

When co-workers work with different sets of information and conflicting personalities and work approaches, it can create tension and lead to misunderstanding and anger. Improving communication techniques and ensuring that

"*Communication is about being effective, not always about being proper.*"

– Bo Bennett

employees follow and share communication protocols can help alleviate the many problems in the workplace. Lack of communication is a very important issue to overcome in the workplace among co-workers. It will not be easy, as they say "as a piece of pie", but it will consist of being real and getting right to the point. When resolving the situations in your workplace that deal with lack of communication, remember to give it time, and motivate the employees properly.

Many co-workers fail to communicate certain issues in the workplace because they can't stand their co-workers, and the job goes undone because of poor communication skills and abilities. Poor communication is an important issue to overcome in the workplace, although it may not always be easy. When resolving the situation in your workplace, remember to give it time, and motivate the employees properly.

Among the most trying elements of poor communication in today's workplace is a lack of information for the proper accomplishment of the tasks necessary within the business. Even in today's information-overloaded society, employees often lack the information they need to do their jobs. They may have the data they require from external supplies, however, it is the information that their supervisors and co-workers have, but have not properly shared, that remains unsaid.

Frequently, this poor communication is a result of the fact that the people with the information are still processing it themselves, and haven't distanced themselves enough from the problem to discover that there are other people around them who will also be requiring that information. Sometimes, the way in which people communicate can actually be the cause of poor communication in workplace.

Employees everywhere must understand that clear and consistent communication is necessary to have a healthy corporate structure. It is absolutely vital to the relationship between an employer and employees. Only through effective communication with one another can you build a strong relationship among employees and employers. Every workplace will face unpleasant experiences and different attitudes that will cause employees one way or another to respond.

When conflict occurs within the workplace, employees must be committed to communicating with their employer in order to resolve the conflict. If the employee chooses not to pursue the grievance, an opportunity exists which will foster negativity, resentment, and bitterness toward the employer. Communication is the vehicle in which tranquility and personal growth can take place for both parties (both the employee and the employer). Every employee must understand that no one is an "island" and that no one can effectively do the job by themselves. We all need each other to run an effective workplace that will cause us to serve our customers to the best of our abilities. We, as employers and employees, must not always focus on the past and faults of others; instead, we must see the possibilities in each other.

A lack of communication in the workplace can lead to such things as gossip, resentment, and high staff turnover. When co-workers fail to interchange thoughts, opinions, or information by speech, writing, or signs, then they fail to use the most effective tool called communication. Everyone working within a business communicates with customers and consumers to make sure that all of the clients' needs are met. Without communication, no work could ever be accomplished. Sometimes, the way in which people communicate can actually be the cause of poor communication in the workplace.

HOW TO EFFECTIVELY COMMUNICATE WITH YOUR EMPLOYEES

Communicating with your employee's is very essential tool to convey certain messages that will help enhance every co-worker, to make sure everyone is on the same page and to keep the line of communicating open at all times. Leaders must understand when it comes to communicating to your employees, don't scream or holler at them; just talk to them with respect in a calm voice. Many times, leaders and co-workers feel they can speak to anyone in such a tone that will demand them to give them the respect they deserve. When someone communicates and talks to anyone with curiosity and with respect, they will get the respect they deserve. It takes time for a person to learn to communicate effectively and learn other people's ways and moods that will teach them how to discern when and how to talk to a person. There will be times that your co-worker will be faced with emotions or sickness, and they don't need to hear any negative communication. Individuals in the workplace are tired of ineffective communication, or leaders and co-workers speaking to them like they are a kid or a nobody. When there is effective communication in workplace, this will generate an environment where an employee feels this is a team, and their ideals and opinions matters. Effective communicating has a purpose in the workplace because it has the potential to change and create the future of your organization. When communication is not spoken effectively, this will become a big barrier that will create an unhappy customers and cause them to become angry because of poor service.

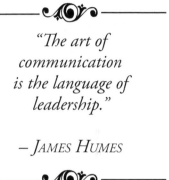

"The art of communication is the language of leadership."

– JAMES HUMES

"Words should be used as tools of communication
and not as a substitute for action."

SOME PEOPLE CAN'T COMMUNICATE WELL

Communication is a skill. Most managers, supervisors, and co-workers, three quarters of the time, find themselves forgetting the importance of communicating with others. There are many people who can't communicate well with others because of fear and a certain level of lack of trust. Think about it. Sometimes, you fear that the other person may simply not agree with you. This would hinder you from speaking up. Nobody likes to have people reject them or disagree with their opinions, so they keep their mouths shut. Perhaps, there isn't enough trust between these persons, trust that the other won't ridicule you for your opinion, or knowing that what you say will be kept private. Trust and fear work inversely. Therefore, with more trust, there is less fear, and with less fear, there is more openness to communicate and express ourselves. I think it is because people are afraid of the other person's reaction to the truth, afraid to speak the truth. And we all know that without trust, communication, and honesty, good relationships fade away. I'm talking about any kind of relationships; marriage, dating, friendship, employees, employer, whatever. To keep things simple, you need to say what is on your mind to the other person. If not, the other person is left to assume what you're thinking and sometimes they can be wrong. For instance, someone, who looks too much into things and analyzes things and don't have all the details, can make things more complicated than they really are.

In the workplace, there are many employees who have a natural flair for communication and a strong sense of confidence or charisma that endears them to others. People who communicate effectively take skills which always begin with confidence. When people display confidence, it shows that they have the ability to attract others like a magnet, because their attitude speaks from the heart.

When using effective communication, one of the most important rules to follow is to look a person directly in the eyes. People who lack confidence tend to avoid eye contact. Avoiding eye contact shows disinterest, or in a worst-case scenario, dishonesty. When two people make eye contact, effective communication is possible. Eye contact also lends credibility to what you say. Many times, there is a breakdown in workplace because of so many reasons. Sometimes, when a person is trying to communicate and it seems hard to say what you want say, try using different communication styles to interact with people. Most employees in the workplace fail to communicate to one another because of certain reasons:

- They don't like the person.
- Their egos get in the way.
- They have no relationship with the person.
- They are having emotional problems.
- They are unskilled on why, how, when and what.
- They always use babbling and gestures.

It very important to communicate to one another clearly to make sure they understand your message that you are trying to convey. There are two reasons why employees must strive for improving communication within the company. First, good communication is vital for building a cohesive staff and minimizing employee turnover. Second, employees' rights are protected more today than ever before, and there is a trend toward judgments and penalties against employers who do not keep pace with employment laws, regulations, and concerns. Good dialogue between management and personnel can resolve many issues in their early stages.

*"Honesty and acceptance
is an ongoing practice,
which is essential to having
clear communication with
our higher nature."*

-UNKNOWN

Always keep in mind that you are an employee working for a company, which means you have a responsibility to that company's interests by communicating well to associates and customers. To put it bluntly, most employees don't like to work around ignorant, bully bosses, "those who think they know it all." They will leave or transfer for better conditions as soon as the opportunity presents itself. Most people don't realize that people are human and have emotions that sometimes get hurt. People become tired of going to work and working hard while others do nothing, "play around", and just "pass the buck" to others. The key to changing that perception is good communication.

When there is a person who is not pulling his weight on the job, you can't allow this type of attitude to be "swept under the rug". There is a proper chain of command that one should go through. Here are the basic steps in solving this type of attitude:

- Go to the person
- Take one or more people with you
- Take it to the boss

When the proper chain of command is taken, this will solve the problem. Employees must treat other employees fairly, and we need to set standards and communicate them early to every stakeholder in an organization. If higher productivity and lower turnover is a goal for you, then effective communication is essential. Sometimes, the communication will need to be on an individual basis, sometimes with groups of people — and, of course, this interaction, especially with so many customers and clients, will often not be a face-to-face communication. With so many different and competing demands upon workplace communication, you really need to plan a sound strategy if you are a senior manager for your workplace. If you aren't a senior manager, but you know that your workplace does not have a communication strategy, then suggest one.

Communication is a deep philosophy, and, therefore, it might take several years to learn effective communication. There are two types of communication: formal and informal. You must not focus on the latter, but there are some etiquettes and rules to be followed while communicating in the formal style. As a co-worker, you must be transparent. Every time we try to communicate with someone, a person will choose to use one of four basic communication styles: assertive, aggressive, passive, and passive-aggressive.

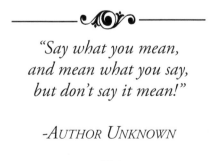

"Say what you mean,
and mean what you say,
but don't say it mean!"

-*AUTHOR UNKNOWN*

CONSEQUENCES OF BAD COMMUNICATION

There are many employees who love to run off at their mouth with others, but when it comes to their work related to achieve their full potential they are bad communicator. The art of communication covers many aspects of the relationship between those in the workplace. In the workplace, there are many individual who have developed a self-centered attitude, and they will chew other people out with their rudeness using harsh, critical, discouraging and hurtful words that causes pain and wounds in people lives. A person's tongue is very dangerous, and it can do much damage when it is out of control (Proverbs 18:21). Then there are many benefits in communicating with your tongue wisely (Proverbs 10:20).

Speech and conversation tells a great deal about one's character (Matthew 12:24). "The ability [to speak] comes so naturally that we are apt to forget what a miracle it is," writes Professor Steven Pinker. "Language is not a cultural artifact that we learn the way we learn to tell time or how the federal government works. Instead, it is a distinct piece of the biological makeup of our brains."

When we understand the power of speech and how it can be positive or negative in a person's life, we will learn to be considerate and evaluate what comes out of our mouths. Speech is a normal means of communicating from one mind to another. Whether we communicate blessing, cursing, comfort, edify, evil speaking, swearing, slander, flattery or to build someone up, one day you will be judged by every word that came out of your mouth (Matthew 12:36). Our thoughts and speech can work against us depending on the frame of mind we are in and what we are thinking about. Speech has tremendous power, and it can be a tool to lift us up, pull us down, wound us deeply, or heal our hearts.

We may not realize that on many occasions our words are uttered without conscious thought, and we also rarely stop and think about what we are saying. Hundreds of words pour out of our mouths every day in the workplace. Our thoughts, opinions, judgments, and beliefs are freely expressed about people and things.

There are many people in the world today who are very opinionated, meaning that they hold very strong opinions on a subject that they refuse to change. Sometimes, this can be bad; these same people are in the workplace, and they can be very dangerous at times. Negative words from our tongues originate from our thoughts, and they are more powerful than our thoughts because, not only do they affect us, but the people around us, too. Another danger with words is that once they are out of our mouths, they can never be taken back.

So should we just say the first thing that comes into our minds—or think about it first? *Seeth thou a man that is hasty in his words? There is more hope of a fool than of him* (Proverbs 29:20). *The heart of the righteous studieth to answer, but the mouth of the wicked poureth out evil things* (Proverbs 15:28). *Wherefore, my beloved brethren, let every man be swift to hear, slow to speak, slow to wrath* (James 1:19).

There are times, as co-workers, you need to confront others about their destructive communication. As employers and employees, you should take a stand when people are trying to entice you to gossip or criticize others that will break down the team and unity. Our words are supposed to build up and encourage other people in a humble way and not express bad things about them (Ephesians 4:29, Titus 3:2). Those in the workplace should believe in those they work around and think well of them, giving them the benefit of the doubt unless their experiences teach them otherwise.

So, remember that the power is not in the words, but in the source of the spirit or attitude of a person. If your heart is not right with God, then you cannot expect to get what you desire and speak. If you are being disobedient to God or refusing to repent over sinful words which cause you to be weak, then don't expect results in your life.

Powerful words from a person with a positive mindset can build up and empower a person through words of encouragement that will bring positive attitudes in your workplace environment.

The wise employer or employee will use restraint in her/his speech and be cautious in what he says when he speaks. He will not exaggerate, fabricate the truth, or harm others when he speaks; rather, he will be careful to speak words that are accurate and that will edify others (Proverbs 17:27).

*"Kindness in words creates
confidence. Kindness
in thinking creates
profoundness. Kindness
in giving creates love."*

-LAO TZU

RULES FOR GOOD COMMUNICATION

People often lack the ability to converse about certain subjects in the workplace that deeply matter to them because they feel they would get into a dispute. As a result, divisive issues are often characterized by destructive debate that can lead to group division and bad attitudes toward one another. That is why, as a group or one-on-one, you need to come together and have a dialogue. The word "dialogue" means we sit and talk with each other, especially those with whom we may think we have the greatest differences. When people in a work setting begin a dialogue, they begin to trade ideas back and forth, evaluate multiple perspectives, and then select the best one. Dialogue, on the other hand, seeks to inform and learn rather than to persuade. In dialogue, people think together. One person gets an idea, another person takes it up, and someone else adds to it. When co-workers begin to participate and make a contribution toward communication, you can create a healthy and open communication environment.

COMMUNICATING CRITICISM

Sometimes, in the workplace, we find ourselves manifesting certain negative attitudes that will separate us from our co-workers. We are told in the Bible to "Love one another," but, of course, some co-workers feel that this is not an easy task.

We as co-workers can have good and strong relationships with one another; we need to recognize those things that have built walls between us. There are two kinds of criticism: constructive and destructive.

When a person criticizes, one of the main purposes that must be taken into consideration is, does the person who is doing the criticizing wants to help or hurt? It is easy to criticize someone you don't like or are not concerned about. A "critical spirit" is an obsessive attitude of criticism and fault-finding, which seeks to tear down others.

This kind of attitude is in the midst of the workplace, and some co-workers don't even care when they degrade and put other people down because they don't like them or they are jealous of them.

Criticism is an attitude based on an expression of disapproval of someone or something based on perceived faults or mistakes. Criticism can be painful and hurtful when someone you work around daily just attacks you for no reason at all with hateful words behind your back. When people speak negative words about you, avoid them at all cost and make sure you don't response back to them with the same negative attitude which will add fuel to the fire in workplace.

"No matter how well you do, no matter how successful you are, they're always going to criticize you."

-TODD BRIDGES

What makes constructive criticism beneficial? I will tell you of my own personal experience. When I first began working as a teenager, I wanted to do an effective job, but an older man saw me working, and he saw me doing the job wrong. I was very zealous, ambitious, and wanting my boss and my team members to know I know a lot about my job. But an old, wise man took me to the side and said, "Never try to work to please people because you are a servant to God and to this organization. So never mimic anyone". He said, "Son, be you and you will feel good about yourself.

His criticism was constructive because I respected him. He came to help me, and he didn't do it publicly, but privately, and his constructive criticism didn't allow me to make a shipwreck of my life, but to mature as a man and on my job, as well.

Constructive criticism is that which is expressed in love to build up, not to teardown—it is always expressed face-to-face, never behind a person's back. The person, who has a critical spirit, usually dwells on the negative, complains, and always seeks flaws rather than good in a person's life.

"Criticism, like rain, should be gentle enough to nourish a man's growth without destroying his roots."

-FRANK A. CLARK

This person with this negative criticism attitude has little control over his tongue and temper and has tendencies to gossip and slander, which Paul said were sins...*worthy of death* (Romans 1:29-32).

There are so many co-workers who love to complain, gossip, and have critical attitudes to stir up strife within the workplace. We must always be alert to those negative, critical employees that love to harass, frustrate and discourage other people. The Scripture warns us not to "give place" to the devil (Ephesians 4:27).

There are other reasons why people criticize one another, and I want to share some of them with you. A chronic fault finder criticizes because this person has a poor self-image. This person feels that spreading rumors about them makes them look bad, but really they make their own selves look bad. Those people, who criticize because they are jealous or just holding a grudge on someone, are just waiting for an opportunity to present itself.

Criticism of other people will eventually spill over into other parts of people's lives. The more we see wrong in other people, the more critical we become at home and with our more intimate friends and relations. This is because gossip and criticism will actually undermine your integrity and ultimately oppress the spirit. This is their way of getting even and satisfying their resentment and jealousy. Some people who critique are those who do it by habit. They have complained, murmured and griped for so long that it has become a habit.

As bosses, supervisors and co-workers, the next time you want to criticize someone, remember that you're damaging that person's reputation. This means that you have an inferiority complex, may be suffering from a lack of self-esteem that you are self-righteous, that you are jealous of the person you are criticizing, feeling a grudge, or possibly just a chronic fault finder. When we criticize others behind their backs, we are spreading workplace scandals, calumny and getting the latest hot news on someone's life and retelling it.

*"A successful man is
one who can lay a firm
foundation with the bricks
that others throw at him."*

-Sidney Greenberg

When it comes to associates communicating to other in authority or certain co-workers, many feel intimidated and don't know how to respond to or approach negative communication in workplace. When you as an employee have a right attitude in the workplace, you display a successful attitude of professionalism. No matter how long you been at your job and how good you are, if you are not trustworthy, you are not to be a good employee. When associates can communicate with skills, this is based on trust.

No matter what people say, if they are not trusted, they are not believed to be good employees. Therefore, in order to have good communication in an organization, you must make sure that you do what you say you are going to do. People, who do what they say they are going to do, are trusted in their workplace; people who don't are not trusted. No matter how good you are at your job, you lose respect from management when you cannot accept constructive criticism. Employee reviews can be stressful; it is human nature to react defensively when we feel misunderstood or when our goals are blocked. With a bit of preparation, proactive strategy and a positive attitude, you can make a disappointing work review work for you, rather than against you. Here are a few ways you can transform your respond from a negative to a positive outcome:

- Envision how you will react in each situation, being proactive.
- Listen carefully for both the negative and constructive criticism.
- Always stay positive and confident in the midst of negative responses.
- Transform constructive criticism into a tool you can use to improve weak areas.
- Always document everything negative that a person says that will support your case.

Negative people rarely contribute much to workplace morale as they wallow in their pessimism, trying to infect other people. However, many people, who are in authority, may feel they have a right to speak to you any kind of way which they think this makes them somebody. Let them know, in a professional way, that God created us the same and they are no better than you. Let them know you respect their title and authority, but if they want you to do something, or if you can improve on anything, please talk to you in a professional way.

*"When people
honor each other,
trust is established,
which further
leads to synergy,
interdependence,
and deep respect.
Both parties make
decisions and
choices based on
what is right,
what is best, what
is valued most
highly."*

— BLAINE LEE

CHAPTER 2

GOSSIP IN THE WORKPLACE

Too many people in the workplace don't know how to limit themselves when it comes to communication and end up encroaching on peoples' private lives. This form of encroachment is dangerous and insidious, and this is called "workplace gossip". Many people in the workplace daily go about sowing seeds of malicious communication about their co-workers. Gossip kills, wounds, and causes hard feelings among co-workers every day. Many co-workers often find themselves using words that will damage and destroy other co-workers' reputations. Gossip is terrible, ugly, and has caused many workplaces to become divided. The negative effects of gossip are strained relationships, mistrust, discontentment, fear for one's life, anger, and decreased productivity. For example, how much time have you wasted, in long conversations, complaining to others about your co-worker who is not as helpful as he could be, or about your partner who is not as loving as you would like them to be?

The word "gossip" is used in the form of slander, backbiting, and scorn. Gossip means to repeat any idle conversation about someone or malicious idle talk to spread information, whether good or bad, to expose someone's failure. According to the dictionary, "gossip" is "when a person habitually engages in idle talk about others", or it is "idle, often sensational and groundless, talk about others". Spreading gossip is condemned by the Word of God.

Gossip is evil, negative, and it is a cowardly attack upon someone's reputation and character. Most employees love to gossip behind other associates' backs because they are not man or woman enough to say to their faces what they feel. Workplace gossip is unproductive. It breeds resentment and becomes a roadblock to effective communication and collaboration. Gossip in the workplace kills camaraderie and morale, and it leaves a toxic environment within the workplace.

"Gossip is rude and juicy
and has caused pain
and emotional wounds
in people lives."

-O.C. Isom

It is disturbing, painful, immature, and shameful how a co-worker can gossip about those with whom they work every day. Gossip is like taking their hands and slapping them in their face or using the legs to kick them in their stomach; gossip is just that bad. Gossip happens when a person doesn't have anything to do.

There is nothing good that comes from boredom, and the Bible says an idle mind is a Devil's workshop. A person who doesn't have something particular with which to occupy him in the workplace will always be tempted to occupy himself by doing mischief. Idleness means you don't have a particular goal in mind and that you can be easily distracted to join up for trouble. Someone has defined gossip as the art of saying nothing, but it always produces nothing in a person's life. Gossip is faster than UPS or Fed-Ex, because gossip seems to travel faster through the sour grapevine of employee or employers.

Idle hands are the devil's workshop; idle lips are his mouthpiece

(PROVERBS 16:27).

Gossip has no virtue. It builds no one's character, solves no problems, heals no wounds, avenges no wrongs, or creates any friends, and it will cause harsh feelings between co-workers. Gossip is the vocalization of potentially destructive facts or rumors about someone, whether true or false, when that person is not present to respond or defend himself.

WORKING IN THE ENVIRONMENT OF GOSSIP

When it comes to gossip in an organization or your workplace; many people use different methods of negative attitudes to get their point across. So many times people seem to be unaware of their methods. Some use innuendoes, hints, references, and associations to make people look bad. In every conversation, some people will leave a negative impression of whomever they were talking about. What any gossiper fails to realize is that people can pick up on body language when they are being talked about. A gossiper in a place of work is so clever they will never be direct, but very indirect. Some co-workers are so afraid in developing a relationship with their co-workers; they will find any chance to avoid any relationship with a team member. What many gossipers fail to realize is that your co-workers have your number. They know when you are lying and when you are spreading rumors to keep up the mess in the workplace.

When the door of gossip is open in the workplace from co-workers, it brings about frustration and hurt feelings. Many co-workers bring about a bad atmosphere in the workplace because of their bad attitudes that they display every day. Those who love to stir up gossip are those who appear to suffer from low self-esteem. Those who gossip in the workplace end up feeling powerless at some point.

What can make a person powerful? When he has some sort of "information" which others may not have. If this person seems to always be in the know about things going on in the office, there is a greater tendency for others to seek her or him out for the latest tidbit. This gives the "gossiper to stir" up the sense of power which they want and need, but is unable to get it in a legitimate manner.

In addition, you have described a person who hints or makes innuendoes, that suggests that they are not even confident enough to make a firm stance on the information being shared. This is also a method of baiting another person. If I toss the line out there with the bait on it and you nibble on it, I know that I have a potential "fish on the line". Also, if I am really lucky, you will take the bait and run with it, and I will then have you "hooked". Either way, I am safe. If you choose not to nibble on the illusory tidbit, I have not exposed myself or my information to you.

In summary, a flower cannot grow in soil that is not right for it. If you and your co-workers allow this type of behavior to continue without addressing and correcting it, you have contributed to creating fertile ground in which this gossiper's negative trait can grow and flourish.

*"Negative people need drama
like oxygen. Stay positive; it
will take their breath away."*

— UNKNOWN

Working and hanging around other associate that gossip is very catching. Gossip is one of the fiendish forms through which employees begin to lie and hurt innocent people who are not present to defend themselves, hence, end up wounding other co-workers for no reason at all. Gossip is an evil attitude that is common and rampant in the workplace all over the world. This evil attitude has further caused havoc and hurtful feelings to the victims in the workplace that have caused hurt and fear that they have to come to work and live with every day. Every person who is married or has ever been in a relationship knows what it is like to say the wrong thing at the wrong time to your spouse or friend. One careless statement can provoke or escalate a conflict that will take weeks, months, or even years to die out.

So, it is true also among people in workplace when someone has a negative attitude of gossip they will speak evil words of anger, sharp words, or aggressive words out of their mouth. People in workplace gossip because they are bored with their lives and they want to create tension in other people lives just to have something to do.

*"The real art of conversation
is not only to say the
right thing at the right
time, but to leave unsaid
the wrong thing at the
tempting moment."*

– DOROTHY NEVILL

Gossip can be a very destructive attitude in places where you work. Corporations depend upon the harmonious relations of workers and departments to avoid strife and dissension. Of course, it can be difficult to completely eliminate gossip from the workplace. Human nature often gets in the way of more sensible behavior. Petty jealousies and rivalries within organizations can lead people to engage in unnecessary gossip. Eliminating gossip from the workplace is possible, to a degree, with a little hard work and planning.

There have been many accusations and rumors in the workplace which have caused hurt and pain in many people's lives as a result of gossip. The unruly mouth of a co-worker has drained people of their enthusiasm and has caused the productivity to suffer. When people are hurt, their emotions get in the way of their work culture, and they won't want to work fast; the work will get done when it gets done.

Many employees do not realize the hurt, the wounds, and the pain they have caused to many other co-workers because they speak words of destruction. That is why people should think before they speak from their hearts. It's been said, "Great minds talk about other people and ideas!" It's also been said, "Weak minds talk about people".

Unfortunately, it appears that most people in the workplace are weak minded, because they are influenced by gossip and speaking evil of others. Many people who gossip to you about others will soon gossip to others about you as well. Gossip is probably the one thing that most of us do every single day. Everyone can admit that they have gossiped or spread rumors in the workplace about someone. Most people gossip to make themselves feel good. They get an ego boost to hear others speak evil about someone. What many associates fail to realize is what you reap you will sow.

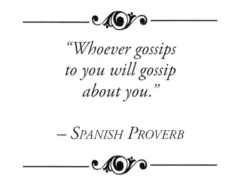

*"Whoever gossips
to you will gossip
about you."*

— *SPANISH PROVERB*

FEATHERS OF GOSSIP
SPREAD IN SOMEONE'S LIFE

Many employees often don't realize that gossip brings about pain and emotional wounds in a person's life and it never goes away. Gossip and slander can leave scars in a person's life for years, and they might never forget the lies that someone has told about them.

A story of gossip was told when an associate on the job worked in a certain department and a certain co-worker began to spread false rumors about him. The co-worker was hurt because it effected his reputation, but he wanted some peace of mind and for the sake of the workplace, he approached the person who had gossiped and spread the rumor about him and told him that he was willing to forgive him. He told the co-worker he was really hurt and emotionally wounded by what he said about him. He then told his co-worker to imagine a box of feathers being thrown in the wind and see if he could find them. The co-worker said it would be impossible to find them. He said that is what it is like when a person has been gossiped about, scarred and emotionally wounded in their life. Sometimes, it is a mental and psychological problem that never goes away. When people spread false rumors, lies, and/or gossip about you within the workplace, it's like putting knives into your back. It is hurtful and painful and may last for years. The moral of the story is don't gossip or spread negative rumors about your co-workers.

*"A real friend's got your
back, while the fake ones
are sticking knives in it."*

- UNKNOWN

In the workplace, emotional trauma will cause a person to lose his self-esteem. On the other hand, kind and encouraging words can build up a person's self-esteem, help them to grow, and can provide the impetus needed to do great and significant things in their life. The choice regarding how we speak to our co-workers has a great impact in the work environment. Forgiveness will heal all wounds, judgments, and grievances. We've all had painful experiences that seem beyond the forgiveness factor. The question is: How long do you want to hold onto the pain? We have a high tolerance for pain. It will last as long as you withhold forgiveness. To be pain free in the workplace, you must forgive everyone for everything they might have done or said about to you — Let it go and move on!

Workplace gossip is too common and it can be devastating to the entire company and to your career as well. Whether you have been the one gossiping or you've been gossiped about, it's important that you learn how to deal with gossip and how problematic it can really be. It doesn't matter whether gossip is true or false; it still has no place at work and must be dealt with.

LISTENING TO GOSSIP IN THE WORKPLACE

Listening is defined as making a statement that says back what the other person just said, exactly or in paraphrase, with no intention of changing anything, adding anything essential, or making any change in the other person's experience. Listening is an important skill in the workplace to make sure a certain order or request from the customer has been fulfilled. Many people listen to gossip when someone approaches them with a negative conversation which if not properly handled turns into gossip.

> *"It's like, Why don't you mind your own business? Solve world hunger. Get out of my closet."*
>
> *– MICHELLE OBAMA*

A big part of listening goes beyond getting the main point and drawing conclusions. To listen empathetically, or with your feelings, means putting yourself in the talker's position without getting emotionally involved. Empathic listening precedes effective feedback because it goes to the root of the concern — the other person's perspective. Many co-workers who listen to gossip have a destructive behavior that brings about division and hatred.

*A dishonest man spreads
strife, and a whisperer
separates close friends*

(PROVERBS 16:28).

Listening is not the same as hearing. Listening is a communication that takes practice. Many people who gossip are good listeners because they love to listen to negative conversations that lead only to confusion in the workplace.

When a person says, "Did you hear what happened?" Listeners should ask themselves how the speaker knows this. To repeat what someone else has said is not evidence; in a court of law, it is nothing but hearsay. Many people will overhear only the partial truth of a conversation they were listening to, and then they will fabricate the partial truth to others about what they have heard.

They never witness the event concerning what was said; they just interpret it incorrectly. It is sinful to believe someone has done wrong when there is little or no tangible evidence. Have you ever played Chinese Whispers? This is a fun game with a serious meaning behind it. Many people sit in a circle, and then the first player whispers a statement into their neighbor's ear. The neighbor then whispers it to the next player — and so on around the circle.

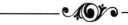

*"Gossip is the art of
saying nothing in
a way that leaves
practically nothing
unsaid."*

—WALTER WINCHELL

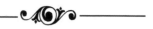

The final player then calls out the message which they have heard. The game shows how rumors get started and how the truth gets distorted along the way as it is passed from mouth to mouth. As a game, it's amusing — but in reality, it paints a true picture of spreading gossip. Many individuals realize that the best way to spread news quickly is to disguise it as a "secret". Many people love to talk about scandal or the downfall of a co-worker.

Gossip is essentially a form of attack, which often arises from an individual's conscious and unconscious fears. For some people, their ostensible commitment "not to gossip" is easily lost in their fears, anxieties, or concerns about what their life might be like if they stopped gossiping. (e.g.; ***Who would I be then? What would I do then? Would I still be one of the guys? Would I have to eat lunch alone? Would I lose all my friends?***)

Some broader definitions of gossip not only relate to "negative" remarks but even extend to "positive" or "neutral" remarks that are focused on making conversation that is centered on the activities/ behaviors of others outside the presence of that person. Stopping the practice of "talking about others" is challenging for many. Why? Many folks just can't be authentic in life. So, many revert to the self-defense mechanism of gossiping, which is a defense mechanism or self-protection device they use so they never have to show up, be vulnerable, or get in trouble. They disclose information about their feelings or emotions, or open up. For these folks, gossiping is a strategy for protecting against revealing one's real or true self. Gossip

"If you haven't got anything to say about anyone, come sit next to me."

— Alice Roosevelt Longworth

is a form of workplace violence. To be free from inflicting this violence on others, we need to explore and heal the split between our outer self and inner self. Only then can we live honest, sincere, and responsible lives in the workplace — and out.

GOSSIP IS LIKE GANGRENE

Many employers and employees are daily caught up in the gossip news of today that makes their day. Many people in the workplace can't wait to run off at their mouth about another person failure and reputation. This is why many people in the workplace mouth are like gangrene. The definition of gangrene is the death or decay of the body tissue that is caused when the blood supply has been cut off or a certain bacterial infection has set up. Gossip is like gangrene...if you don't cut it off it can kill you or give you a bad name in the workplace. Many co-workers don't realize how running off at the mouth can do great harm to workplace environment. Our societies an even in the workplace today are viewed as "television soap opera". Employee everyday make it their business to gossip about someone and to make them look bad and to assassinate their good name and reputation.

"Reputation is what men
and woman think of us;
Character is what God
and angels know of us."

— THOMAS PAINE

CONFIDENTIALLY IN WORKPLACE

When it comes too confidentially in the workplace; in order to build and maintain trust, there must be an honest relationship between your customers, clients, and employees. Confidentially places a duty on employees and employers not to disclose any information with anyone without their consent. Confidentiality is the right of an individual patient to have personal, identifiable medical information kept private. In other words, confidentiality means that whatever is said or shown to me it will stay with me. I would not share the information with another co-worker or friend. Nor would I document that information anywhere.

It is the employee's responsibility to treat all the information in the workplace with care and caution and respect the person private. An employee should be prudent enough not to disclose any information that the organization considers sensitive and confidential, to a third party, whether it is a co-worker, friend or relative unless the employee has permission from proper authority. Every employee should know what files or materials he/she is permitted to access in the office and he should adhere to that. There should be no reason that any files be shown to anyone without proper permission. If for any reason it does get in the wrong hands, it can be considered as a breach of confidentiality which may cause the employee to be fired.

"Confidentiality is a virtue of the loyal, as loyalty is the virtue of faithfulness."

— EDWIN LOUIS COLE

When it comes to confidentiality every employee should beware not to expose any information about anyone personal affairs outside of work. Employees must understand, any personal or professional information about an employee, application form, reference, health issues or salary should be confidential. We this is abuse it can lead to discrimination in the workplace. Only staff members of the HR department who require the data for certain purposes should be given access to the personal files of employees.

Finally, while confidentiality in the workplace involves the way in which employee records are handled and maintained, it also involves employees being taught from day one what conversations are allowed so everyone within the organization is fully protected. This creates a friendly working environment that people enjoy, which equates to dedication and higher production. Keeping employee information safe is not just the law but also the way to run a highly profitable business.

WORKPLACE SNITCH

We all know that the one thing which a person learns in a group setting is: "Nobody likes a snitch or tattletale." But many co-workers find it very hard to comprehend, and eventually these pint-sized snitches become integrated into the workforce where they make their colleagues' and managers' lives difficult. Snitching and being a tattletale is bad for employee morale and camaraderie; who wants to be working around people who snitch and stab you in the back? Snitching and tattletale turns into "brown nosing" to other co-workers and to the boss on the verge of hoping they can get a promotion on the job while making other co-workers' look bad. However, here are some ways you can spot a snitch or tattletale. It's a good idea to stay away from them.

- They always want revenge if something has been taken away from them.
- They always show disrespect and jealously toward other co-workers.

- They will use squealing and other negative strategies for ascending the corporate ladder.
- They hang around with each other so they can speak negatively about someone.
- They say things to other that sometime end up in an altercation.

They complain to management to tell on others by using childish complaints against other co-workers. So when these low-down snitches or tattletales are in your presence speak to them but avoid their negative comments about others. People view a snitch or tattletale as people with low self- esteem and they have no respect among their co-workers.

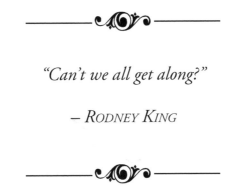

"Can't we all get along?"

– RODNEY KING

HOW TO DEAL WITH THOSE WHO SNITCH AND TATTLETALE

Tattling is one of the most popular and most common negative attitude behaviors among siblings, co-workers and church members. This type of attitude in many places has been overlook and not dealt with properly. My mom told me once son never be a tattletale because this type of attitude will cause people to dislike you. Tattling reigns as destructed attitude in the workforce that many co-workers are involved in every single day. It is being done in hopes to make someone life miserable and to destroy someone reputation. When those in the workplace understand that a person who is a tattletale is someone who will loves to backbite, gossip, backstabbed or betray your trust. A person who is a tattletale in workplace always stirs up fire among other co-workers in the workplace. The attitude of being a tattletale in workplace is a power and dangerous attitude that always bring about division and hurt feeling. Seriously when a person loves to tattletale they are very immature and they love to stir up drama and they want special attentions.

"We do it legally, but we play dirty the same way they do when they go after drug dealers. We are called snitches and tattletale."

– Anonymous

Most people who are tattlers have so much pride they just want to expose someone failure that will make them look bad and make themselves look good. I've always seem co-workers tattling on other co-workers with the intent to get them in trouble so they can get next to the boss or supervisor. Some co-worker have negative attitude because they despise or hate their own team members who they work around daily. So many bosses and co-workers love to destroy the unity of their team at the expense of tattling on someone to make their reputation look bad. It is a shame in so many workplaces to experience gossip and people are tattling that cause people to suffer the consequence of being hurt and emotional wounded. Many co-workers need to shut their mouth and find ways to bring about unity among your team instead of division. If you get tempted to "tattle" on your co-worker ask yourselves do I want someone tattletale about me. So next time your co-worker make a mistake, please don't run to your boss or supervisor and let them know what she/he messed up. All ways use their problems as an opportunity to work as a team to solve the problem together. Working as a team is very important in the workplace or for any business because this kind of attitude always get the job done working as a team effort.

*"People have been known
to achieve more as a result
of working with others
than against them."*

- DR. ALLEN FROMME

Try to avoid this type of people as much as possible, and I'll assure you; they will quit peddling their tales to you. When people do not listen to them and participate in the tattletales, they do not want anything to do with them. Yes, they probably will call you a weird-do but that's okay we know who the real weirdo is...don't we?

Trust is a very important key component of any successful company or team, and it only takes one gossiping employee to kill the atmosphere. Remember: A work force or team built on trust will be happier, more productive, and more effective. So don't let one person ruin the work dynamic for everyone.

STRATEGIES FOR DEALING WITH TATTLETALES

Tattletale is a hard habit for some people to break, but fortunately, there are a few steps that employees can take to protect themselves from trifling or unjust accusations. They can also do a few things to help nip a tattletale in the bud or minimize the damage that one can do to a team. Keep tight-lipped. Don't give devious co-workers ammo or information they can later use against you. Avoid their dervish conversation. Don't listen to people who aim at bringing down fellow co-worker don't fight fire with fire.

Whatever you do, don't retaliate by gathering unflattering information about other employees and passing it on. Don't lose your temper. Many divisive employees thrive on attention, and if you angrily confront a suspected informant, you're letting him or her win. Always give positive feedback. When someone talk about a person negative always reply back with a positive answers.

Having a tattletale as a co-worker will cause you unnecessary grief, they may be adults but they have a childish mind. Some people like to not only spread gossip in the office, but also report big and small issues to the manager. Many employees think if they inform the boss or supervisor by being a tattletale this will cause them to get a better job, raise or to be notice. Working with these types of people with these kinds of attitude will make your life miserable in your team environment. What many tattletales fail to realize that you will reap what you sow because you create an environment of accountability?

"We don't have to expose evil people; they will expose themselves."

- ANTOINETTE GANT

HOW TO AVOID GOSSIP IN THE WORKPLACE

A negative work environment is a less productive work environment. Gossip in the workplace can create an uncomfortable atmosphere not only for the person who is gossiping but for everyone in the workplace. It is important that every employer and employee remembers to seize every opportunity not to spread gossip with their co-workers. Rather, use your tongue and every opportunity to foster unity and to build unity among one another.

"There is a right way and a wrong way to communicate in workplace, choose the right way."

HERE ARE SOME BASIC TIPS ON HOW TO DEAL WITH GOSSIP

Analyze the source of the gossip, the person involved, why they always bring the gossip, what's in it for them, and why they love to assassinate a certain person's character. Then, while you are listening to them, ask yourself how this will benefit you and them as well. Don't take pleasure in something that will degrade someone or spread negative information about another person.

Evaluate the information you share with co-workers. There are some things that are better left unsaid than to be shared with those you only socialize with in the workplace. You may think that what you are sharing with a friend and the information you are sharing is harmless to you and others, while someone may see it as the latest scoop and begin to spread gossip. People will hear this information and will twist and change it as it is passed along.

Limit your association in the workplace by not gossiping. Some people tend to get thrills from spreading gossip, and you will have less of a chance of being the original source of the gossip. Remember how easy it is to fall prey to guilt by association.

Walk away from employees who love to formulate gossip in the workplace. Again, not giving power to the source of gossip will help extinguish the spread of negative information at the place of work.

Confront the person who is gossiping. Ask them why they believe this information should be spread around the office or department and what personal gain they will derive from it. Sometimes, the best defense against gossip is to have a strong offense in not tolerating the action of gossip. Let the gossiper know that you are not comfortable discussing the gossip they are fueling. You can even say, "Hey, I do not like talking about other people's private business, because I am pretty sure I would not like them talking about me."

GOOD GOSSIP IN THE WORKPLACE

When we defined gossip, we said it is an exchange of personal information about the absence of a third party that can be either evaluated positively or negatively. That is, gossip can be prepared good or evil; it is up to the person who presents it. Good gossip, in the original sense of the word, can become a glorious instrument for spreading the truth in the workplace and in the office that will build morale among employees. It is interesting to note that the first meaning of the word gossip is to "chat or rehearse". Employees and Employers must spread and rehearse good and positive news among their employees to bring about a better work environment for co-workers and a productive rapport.

It appears that gossiping is one of the greatest challenges to overcome in the workplace. When we really perform self-examination and take a moment to listen to ourselves gossip, it can positively impact our behavior. We must really comprehend that gossip is distasteful! It is poisonous!

It contaminates our spirit! Gossiping is sin — period! Gossiping in the workplace contributes nothing of value for the betterment of others or the company. Scripture says in the Bible:

As co-workers, we must choose to believe the positive about someone, because everyone has the potential to contribute to the betterment of others in the workplace, but this is more of a personal choice as it is up to an individual to make personal choice. If anyone chooses to be a part of the workforce, you must not allow gossip to undermine your efforts and cause you to destroy the teamwork.

HOW TO AVOID GOSSIP IN THE WORKPLACE

Eradicating gossip at the workplace is not an easy task, it begins with yourself and upper-level management. Present a professional image by being cheerful, courteous, and pleasant. But when you are faced by gossiping employees trying to gossip about colleagues, tell them that you prefer to leave personal issues alone. Some people may not even realize that they are gossiping because they see it as chatting or exchanging information. Someone who is mature or a supervisor should make them aware that this will not be tolerated. Open communication helps to stifle rumors and misinformation. Allowing gossip in the workplace is like encouraging your employees to swim with sharks. Cutting right to the chase, real leaders don't participate in gossip, and likewise they don't tolerate gossip from others. Gossip destroys trust, undermines credibility, and is one of the greatest adversaries of a healthy corporation culture. With the emotional distress associated with gossip can be dealt

"Connect to your goodness within that will cause you to see the good quality in a person"

– O.C. Isom

with fairly easily, the political discord that can erupt in an organization can be nothing short of disaster.

In today's world where gossip is the hallmark of the day, I will share my thoughts on how to control gossip in workplace. Question is this: as a leader, do you want to create a culture of doubt or a culture of leadership? If what you desire as an executive and an example is to have a healthy, thriving, and productive company, it is essential that you curtail office gossip. Gossip is one of the most divisive undercurrents pervading the smooth running of an organization as it allows for the unnecessary dispersion of negative innuendo for the pleasure of a few, and to the detriment of many…Show me a person that participates in gossip and I'll show you someone who cannot be trusted and have an emotional mental problem. People who participate in gossip often times view their activity as being politically savvy, when in fact gossip is the insecure attitude and rank of amateur character of a person and his/her profession.

I personally resolve that if I do not have anything good to say about a person, then I simply will not say anything at all. I believe that it is better to keep silent than to slander. Therefore, when the time comes to keep silent, I will seize the moment to search for good even in the gossiper.

CHAPTER 3

ATTITUDE IN THE WORKPLACE

With the current American economy in a recession, it can be difficult to maintain a positive attitude in the workplace. In fact, sometimes it can seem like *Mission Impossible*. Instead of falling victim to the negative work attitudes that surround you, make an effort to buck the trend. Look for the good in your co-workers and your workplace. By learning how to communicate with co-workers effectively, you will gain recognition as a force of positive attitude in the workplace. Here are some initial steps one can take to communicate with co-workers effectively:

- Have a pleasant smile.
- Revive yourselves daily with (prayer).
- Volunteer your time.
- Avoid negative co-workers.
- Appreciate one another.
- Stop blaming others.

Your attitude in the workplace can be an example or reference point on how others in your workplace look at you and feel about you as a co-worker. A first impression can be a hard thing to shake, especially if it's a bad one. In other words, once you have gotten a workplace reputation as being lazy, a gossiper, a whiner, or other negative tags, it can be hard to get rid of them. Think of someone you've worked with who perhaps didn't work as hard as you expected them to, and then think about how you felt every time you had to work with them. False perceptions are often interpreted as reality, and once people get an idea in their heads about someone or something, it can be difficult to get them to think differently. In my experience, your attitude in the workplace can sometimes define you more than the work you actually produce if your co-workers come to see you as someone who is reliable, competent, intelligent, and someone on whom they can rely. One of the worst feelings you can ever have, is having to work with people who don't seem to care and who don't appear to pull their own weight.

These negative attitudes do exist in the workforce today, and some attitudes are not pleasant. We were all created with emotions, and sometimes co-workers allow their emotions to get the best of them, which causes drama in the workplace and in people's lives.

Emotions are feelings on the inside caused by pain or pleasure trying to move you in a certain direction. Please understand that God gave you emotions to feel compassion and love toward Him and others. Many times, co-workers channel their negative emotions toward others who have caused them to act a certain way.

A person's emotions will often try to influence and determine their decisions and make them cause certain problems in people's lives. When co-workers have ungodly attitudes, the words they allow to come out of their mouths sometimes are unreal.

It is very important that positive attitudes be implemented in the workplace. When there are bad attitudes in the workplace, it will lead to poor work cultures, which, in turn, affect production in a negative way. Bad attitudes have threatened many people and customer service in the workplace. Bad attitudes can spread like a virus from individual employees or through departments, and they can infect the entire organizations because of one bad attitude virus that spreads and, in no time, causes an epidemic. Productivity suffers, and so do individual workers.

It all starts with attitude! A positive attitude is a priceless possession for personal fulfillment and career success. It is also an essential element for creating a positive rapport around the workplace. It's what really matters. When we think about the basic elements of human relationships, we think primarily about the attitude we each bring to relationships, whether they are personal or professional in nature. What is the first thing you remember about someone you meet? Chances are — it's their attitude!

Today, in the workplace, situations have changed dramatically. Companies are either "downsizing", "rightsizing", "merging", or "being acquired". Thousands of people, who thought their lives were secure through retirement, are now suddenly vulnerable. Some will become unemployed, and those who remain will wonder when *their* turns will come.

These are the kind of circumstances that can defeat you — if you let circumstances dictate your life. That's what happens to a lot of people. For others, the circumstance becomes an opportunity for getting where they want to go. One of the challenges facing management and co-workers today is dealing with difficult people — those who have negative attitudes. It is important to note that a person with a negative attitude has the same power to influence others as that person with a positive attitude. The difference appears in the results.

Positive attitudes in the workplace have many benefits, including:

- Improved communications skills
- Promotion of teamwork

- Increased morale
- Increased productivity

The opposite is true for negative attitudes. Many co-workers come to work only to dismantle teamwork, increase stress, and cripple productivity. The big difference between the winners and the losers is often attitude. The salesperson who sells more, the manager who inspires her people, the manufacturing supervisor who sets the tone for everyone around them, are all good examples of what attitude does for you and for everyone around you. Attitudes exist in the workplace for many reasons. Here are a few reasons why some co-workers have a negative attitude in the workplace:

- They hate their job.
- They bring their problems to work.
- Favoritism
- Prejudice
- Lazy co-workers

Having a positive and right attitude is expected from everyone in the workplace. Attitudes are expressed by your actions, better known as "your behavior". So, basically, if you show the right behavior in the workplace, then you are also showing the proper attitude. It is also said that workplace attitudes are simply the way a person is thinking. For example, if the people in your workplace were to portray positive attitudes and behaviors, then everyone would be in a better work environment. Finally, a significant change in a person's way of thinking is the only way to make a significant change in their life, as well at their workplace.

DISPLAY EXCELLENCE IN THE WORKPLACE

It's not surprising when we look at the number of immature people we have in the workplace nowadays. The tantrums, yelling, drama, and the throwing of things and outright expression of emotions that is detrimental to work and the office environment though unconventional is common in most offices. To be mature at work is learning how to display professionalism that brings about an environment of self-awareness to be aware of how to communicate with excellence with your peers, associate and customers.

If you want to bring excellence in the workplace, learn to adjust, modulate, and direct your emotions. Think before acting and understand that your actions can affect the rest, especially team members who works closely with you. How can someone approach you if they feel you are in a foul mood every day? How effective and efficient can you be then? How will people around you achieve excellence in the workplace? When you are open to new ideas, you gain more opportunities to display excellence in every area of the workplace.

"Never settle in any things you set your mind to do, embrace your challenges, ignore your fears and excel having the attitude of excellent"

- O.C. Isom, II

It's just something you never noticed due to all the drama from immaturity. It is something you did not realize and the time to reflect upon your actions. Maturity allows you to understand that **passion** and **persistence** to pursue your goals at work, beyond monetary returns, gives you a purpose of service in life. With passion, persistence, and patience, excellence can be achieved in the workplace. You, as an individual, can inspire the rest to show their best at work without even

"The more you need your Boss, Supervisor or Customer the less they need you."

trying too hard because you would have already created the environment to do so. Excellence in leadership is not a trait only for the top of the organization, but a skill to be developed in everyone throughout the organization. If any one person cannot lead the tasks for which they are responsible, they are likely not needed. Many co-workers have the attitude when the cat is away the mouse will play, in other words when those who are not in charge are absent, employees tend to play around, refuse to work, and take longer breaks.

When you behave and act maturely at work, you become discerning. You know how to carry out the workload in the case of a crisis or when there is staff shortage. Just like a mother who pats and encourages a child. A small act, but it helps the child build confidence. Maturity brings excellence in the

"We need to internalize this idea of excellence. Not many folks spend a lot of time trying to be excellent."

– Barack Obama

workplace because it allows you to respect and appreciate the work others do, and not look at it as an action to gain favors. More importantly, ego is parked aside because of the level of maturity as a professional.

Maturity must exist if you want to have excellence in the workplace. A workplace that is filled with people who are mature, asks how things can be done better. They do not ask why it is not done my way. Parking ego aside, more work can be done better and more efficiently. This success can only come when maturity is an element and everyone knows what is expected of them, hence, resulting in excellence.

Dedication to perform will require a desire to complete whatever task is at hand, knowing that the work serves a purpose. Dedication is the willingness to go the extra mile and to commit to what a person says they will do. Dedication leads to thorough work production and adequate use of time. A person who is dedicated to their work will do the best job possible and take pride in their performance, punctuality, and accountability. Excellence starts with a person love for what they do. That why it is important for the organization to use people who are skill to influence the members of your team. Coaching you to treat your people well by using these skills is one of the dominant themes that will cause your employees to experience excellence.

Integrity is a quality that is earned with time, self-discipline, and through consistency. A person must set high standards for himself in order to be a person of integrity. By setting high standards, a person is less likely to compromise their beliefs and values. A person with integrity performs to the best of their ability even when nobody is watching, because they know it is not about who is watching, it is the principle of being truthful and productive because they are dedicated and fulfilling to a purpose.

Excellent work performance is characterized by consistent ability to be where a person says they will be and when they say they will be there. Punctuality shows a person can be counted on. Accountability is important for maintaining long lasting work relationships and excellence. The person with a record of accountability and punctuality is more often than not acknowledged for this when it comes for promotion, salary or raise. A company is far more willing to invest in someone they know will be at work today, tomorrow, and the next day.

Cultivating workplace excellence strengthens business, families, and society. Viewing the employee as high leverage variable and taking measures to alleviate their stress goes a long way in terms of helping organizations' compete successfully through improved performance, reduced costs, and enhanced profitability.

To the managers, they should bear in mind that employees are our most valuable assets and providing them with flexibility and work balance has allowed us to attract and retain the brightest and the best. Excellence may bring to mind unmatched performance, unusual expertise, or consistent high-quality performance. In our minds, we often associate excellence with talent. To be the best, surely you have to be gifted, right? Experience has taught me that talent, while important, in no way explains excellence. In fact, the primary pathway to excellence has three main steps, none of which depends on talent. You must have passion and caring, really looking at the big picture to create excellence in your performance. You must developed discipline; passion will not take you to excellence where there is no discipline or practice. You will

"A group becomes a team when each member is sure enough of himself and his contribution to praise the skill of the others."

— NORMAN HIDLE

always be honored because of your conduct because you have the traits of passion and discipline. Team leadership and team building go hand in hand. A successful leader is like a potter whose work is to mold a fragmented work environment into a cohesive one so their workers may achieve excellence. The job of the leader is to encourage teamwork and inculcate:

- Positive thinking
- Be there for them
- Be honest with them and should not make bias decisions
- Keep boosting their morale and confidence
- Always be there for your customers

Team members should always praise each other's performances and be open to take challenges and learn new things that will cause each other to arrive at excellence. Every team in every workplace must learn how to increase their performance by getting every associate to bond and work together. Many corporate companies across the world have begun team building activities to improve the performance of their employees.

GOOD AND BAD
CUSTOMER SERVICE IN THE WORKPLACE

Customer service is a part of any business. Unfortunately, service is sometimes quite bad. There are a few possible reasons you may experience bad customer service and employee attitudes when dealing with a business representative; you can combat some of these problems with good business practices. Poor customer service is the failure to respond to customer queries and complains in regards to your product. These conditions may be caused by unmotivated employees and lack of proper organizational structures.

Sometimes, understanding what the opposite of a concept is can be the key to grasping the knowledge you need. If you know what poor customer service looks like, then it is easier to recognize great customer service strategies when you see them. If you can avoid customer service pitfalls, you must be able to create a knowledge that will cause good customer service experience that keeps customers coming back. We all know that a positive tone and language are highly important when it comes to good customer service, but many retailers still use phrases that may give the wrong image and negatively impact our customers' shopping experience.

"Customers don't expect you to be perfect. They do expect you to fix things when they go wrong."

– DONALD PORTER V.P., BRITISH AIRWAYS

As customer service you should never treat your customer bad. Your customer is the one that keeps your company in business and make sure you keep your job by keep giving you the business. When you display any form of negativity toward a customer this is a turn off and you could cause your customer never to come back to your place of business. Here are some positive sayings for employees:

- When a customer asks you where a certain product is, never tell them, "It is not my job".

- Never allow your customer to see you with a bad attitude; it will be a turn off.

- Customers may be mad. Just tell them, "Calm down; we will get to you as soon as we can".

- Make sure you treat every customer with curiosity and respect.

- Always talk professionally to your customer.

- Never point and tell your customer, "It is over there". Show or take them where they should go.

- If you are out of a product, let your customer know when it will be in.

- Always have a good smile on your face.

- Make sure you go the extra mile for your customer.

- Make sure to tell them, when they leave, "Have a nice day".

When any associate displays poor customer service, this kind of attitude is not acceptable. When any associate hears or sees bad customer service, go to them and show them how to do it properly because a bad attitude will cause the company to lose money. Don't confront your colleague about the way they have treated the customer. Rather, take them out for lunch or have a cup of coffee together. Get to know your colleague and find out how they are. Usually personal problems reveal themselves in the way people treat others. By being a friend and showing some concern for your colleague, you can help them bear their problems better.

Then, as you become a better friend, you will earn the right to encourage them to be more polite or patient with customers. There will be time you will have an angry customer. Let them know you are sorry that we couldn't meet their expectation; just listen to them showing them that you care. Build relationships with people and influence them from a position of support. Then there will be less danger to your company and your job from poor customer service.

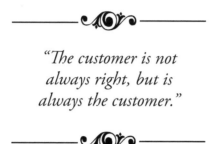

"The customer is not always right, but is always the customer."

Good Customer Service

These days, many business owners understand the importance of their employees projecting a professional image to customers, particularly at the first point of contact. By creating a good first impression by being welcoming and friendly is a very good customer service skill to have and use in any business situation. It is important to have employees trained and knowledgeable in the products and in good customer service. To understand what is customer service, it is a series of activities designed to enhance the level of customer satisfaction – that is, the feeling that a product or service has met the customer expectation."

Your business would not exist without customers. And if you have customers, you have to have customer service. Everybody talks about the importance of good customer service, but few seem to follow through on it. Customers have more options than ever before - and feel less loyalty. They want products and services fast, cheap,

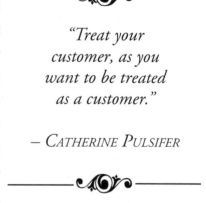

"Treat your customer, as you want to be treated as a customer."

– CATHERINE PULSIFER

quick from whoever will provide them. That means that the competitive advantage is now in your ability to KEEP customers and build repeat business. And the email mindset makes it even easier for customers to spread out their dissatisfaction. Make Customer Jones angry and chances are you've got a nasty rumor going around to ten of his colleagues that you're a lousy firm to do business with.

Good customer service is no longer enough. It has to be superior, WOW, unexpected service. In a nutshell, it means doing what you say you will, when you say you will, how you say you will, at the price you promised - plus a little extra tossed in to say, "I appreciate your business". Even the best business ideas fail because they lack in the area of customer service. Customer service is the backbone and starting point for any successful business. How do businesses succeed? Ask any business owner and they will tell you because of their customers. Ask any customer why they visit one business over another and your answer will likely be customer service.

The following are the top five tips for good customer service.

1 - You Value Your Customers, Now Let Them Know It

Your customers want to feel as though you value them. They want to believe that when they contact you for any reason that you are going to be in tune with them, giving them attention, listening to what they have to say, and being respectful all at the same time. For a short period of time, your customer, when they contact or visit you, wants to feel like they are the most important person in your world at that very moment.

2 - Understand That Time is of Essence

Your customer's time is just as valuable as your own. When dealing with customers, make sure that you do everything you can to minimize their wait time, answer their questions, and refrain from passing the buck. If there is a question that you cannot answer, you should immediately find out who can answer it and refer the customer to that person. Refrain from passing the customer from person to person in efforts to find the answer; send them to the right person the first time, if at all possible.

3 - Employees That Know Their Business

There is nothing worse in customer service than a customer who gets a sales person or operator who has no clue as to what they are talking about. You want to make sure that you, yourself, as well as any person working with you that must deal with customers, have extensive knowledge of your entire business. This means every element from prices to products to services and all the way down to promotions, guarantees, as well as policies.

> *"A customer is the most important visitor on our premises. He is not dependent on us — we are dependent on him."*
>
> *– Author Unknown*

4 - Remain Cordial Even in the Face of Anger

In customer service, you should expect to deal with difficult and demanding customers. However, you should have the ability to deal with these types of customers without losing your own cool, your respect, your attention, and your listening skills. If you are nice to them, chances are their attitudes will change while dealing with you. Make sure that you make every effort to resolve their problems and keep them as a customer in the future.

5 - Remember Why You Have a Job

Let's face it; if there were no customers, you wouldn't have a job, it is as simple as that. The customer is the total basis to your business; without them, it wouldn't exist. Therefore, you have to keep them happy and be sure that you are providing them with good customer service at all costs. This means you need to answer their questions, help them in finding what they need, solve their problems, and meet their demands in a quick, but professional fashion.

When you want to provide good customer service in your business, the above five tips are the elements you need to be looking at and considering. You, as an employee, should always be positive, have a smile on your face, and always respond to customer requests in a timely manner. Clients need to know that you value them and their business. The business motto is, "The customer is always right, even when he's not".

If you keep them waiting or forget about something you were supposed to do for them, you won't keep your clients for very long. Always follow up on your customers and contact them when you have finished the job or after the purchase is complete and ask them what their experience was like, and if they were satisfied. If they were happy with everything, great…ask for a referral. If not, try to make things right. When you build a business that will define good customer service, you are laying the foundation of a company that will also define success.

POOR HYGIENE IN THE WORKPLACE

Poor hygiene is known to be unacceptable in our culture, with good reason. People do not want to be around someone who smells badly or is not clean. Poor hygiene is known to have health effects as well, so it is important to keep yourself clean. Practicing good hygiene will prevent the spread of illness and

"Keep your own house and its surroundings pure and clean. This hygiene will keep you healthy and benefit your worldly life."

SRI SATHYASAI BABA

disease. Washing your hands periodically throughout the day will prevent the spread of colds, flu, and other ailments. When an employee has poor hygiene it will make him or her feel self-conscious about his or her body, leaving him or her to concentrate on that instead of his or her work or customers. Good hygienic habits will make you feel better about yourself and your body.

When asked what problem seems the most difficult and delicate to handle among business or in the workplace among employees is the sloppy appearance and poor hygiene among staff. While this may seem outside the job description of the business manager, it is too often a reality that must be dealt with. Potential clients often judge company validity by the appearance of its staff and sadly deals have been lost due to poor appearance and hygiene. Many employees use too much perfume, which causes some people to have an allergic reaction to it. Employees must not wear wrinkled, smelling, unkempt clothing that does not fit in with the culture or office environment; then it can create a bad impression and project a poor image for the business in the eyes of customers.

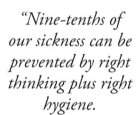

"Nine-tenths of our sickness can be prevented by right thinking plus right hygiene.

— HENRY MILLER

If you own a business with strict OSHA laws on employee hygiene, it is imperative that you enforce them with your employees. If you do not follow these laws, you will be liable. And you risk having your business shut down for good or dealing with the guilt (and perhaps legal effects) of making your customers ill. Personal hygiene encompasses all of the daily routines that help keep your body clean. This includes regular healthy habits of brushing your teeth, washing your hair, washing your hands, cleaning your body with soap and water, wearing deodorant when possible and keeping your clothing clean. When people don't learn these habits, or they become overlooked, certain consequences may develop ranging from social problems to potentially serious diseases.

BODY ODOR

One of the first and most prominent consequences in the workplace is bad hygiene or body odor. Body occurs due to the interaction of bacteria and sweat produced by the apocrine glands. As bacteria thrive in unwashed sweat, over time their byproducts produce the smell commonly associated with body odor. Body odor may also come from poor bathroom habits, resulting in feces or urine odor. Make sure you take daily bath or showers and stay odorless free in the workplace.

BAD BREATH

Bad breath proves another easily recognizable consequence of poor hygiene in workplace. It commonly develops from not regularly brushing and flossing your teeth. Bad breath results because of two main reasons. First, bacteria thrive on particles of food that can stick to your teeth; as the bacteria digest this food, their byproduct results in odor. Many times a person can develop a gum disease infection which also causes bad order in the mouth. Food can also get stuck in your teeth and rot over time, producing a foul odor. Make sure go to the dentist and carry breath mints.

You should present your employee hygiene policy in writing to each of your newly hired workers. This policy should clearly explain expectations of employee hygiene. For example, you might include when the employees must wash their hands, when they should wear gloves, when they should wear a hairnet, and what clothing is and is not acceptable to wear. You might also wish to ban the use of cologne since the scent can be irritating to certain customers and patients.

Once you have created an employee hygiene policy, present this information to your employees. In addition, they should sign a paper documenting that they have received a copy of it. Then, when an issue does arise, consult this policy to decide the action you will take in response to your employee's lack of proper hygiene. If your business involves working with other people, like in nursing, you also have the right and duty to demand that your employees wear clean clothing and that they wash their hands frequently and keep a good odor about themselves.

Delivering the "sorry, but you smell" message must be done delicately, tactfully, and in private. Keep the following in mind. Don't dance around the issue or avoid directly saying what the problem is. Tell the employee upfront that he/she has a body odor problem that must be dealt with. If the employee's offensive body odor continues even after you've discussed it, inform him/her that coming to work unclean or unkempt is unprofessional and disrupts productivity. Put the employee on notice that he/she must come to work clean smelling and appropriately groomed immediately. If he/she doesn't, take appropriate disciplinary action. For instance, you could send the employee home (with pay) to freshen up and issue a written warning.

DEVELOPING A POSITIVE ATTITUDE IN THE WORKPLACE

Your thoughts and emotions, day in and day out, can affect all aspects of your life. Learning to be mindful of your "internal dialogue" will help you recognize thought patterns and how they may be affecting the way you handle the situations of daily living. Many people have found that when they tune in to their internal dialogue, much of it is negative. Thoughts like, *I could never do that*, and, *What if I fail?* These can seriously impact the way you behave.

The stress associated with attachment to this negative internal dialogue, in turn, affects every aspect of your life. When we are stressed, certain hormones are produced by the body. When released infrequently, these hormones are harmless, but when produced continuously, they can cause serious damage. Cardiovascular disease is caused, in part, by the continuous bombardment of stress hormones and by the arterial damage caused by the free radicals created in the process.

Noted authors such as Elwood Chapman and William McKnight say, "The attitude you bring with you every day will significantly affect what you can see, what you can do, and how you feel about it." We all know what a positive attitude sounds like, but how can we define it? Simply stated, Chapman and McKnight describe it as the way you look at things mentally — your mental focus on the world. It's never static; it's always in flux — the result of an ongoing process that's dynamic and sensitive to what's going on.

Events, circumstances, and messages — both positive and negative — can affect your attitude. A positive attitude can be infectious! Let's face it — no one can be positive all the time! What we do know is that a positive attitude makes problem solving easier, and the more you expect from a situation, the more success you will achieve (The High Expectancy Success Theory).

There is no place where your positive attitude can be more appreciated by others than where you work. How does a positive attitude about diversity impact the world of business? A major change has taken place in recent years in the workforce: The generational and cultural mix of employees has become more diversified. The performance standards are the same, but the workforce mix is different. Business is complex and competitive — with comparable resources, including people. People with a positive attitude are looking up and forward and are more likely to work to higher standards of quality, safety, and productivity — individually and as a team. All employees and employers must develop a can-do attitude that was inspired by President Barack Obama. He wanted to inspire his followers to believe that all things are possible. I believe this quality is essential in every leader and co-worker; to portray a can-do attitude. A can-do attitude inspires, and reminds people to believe in a greater future within their workplace when they developed a positive mindset.

Working near a person with a positive attitude is an energizing experience; he/she can change the tone and morale of the department and make others feel more upbeat. Sometimes, the reason people lack a positive attitude is simply — they don't realize that they have a negative one!

"The positive thinker sees the invisible, feels the intangible and achieves the impossible."

—Unknown quotes

A positive workplace is about the people and their positive outlook about their work and the organization that makes the business thrive. The war for talent exists. Do we want to hire and retain people with positive or negative attitudes? The answer is obvious: Hire for attitude; the mechanics of the job can be taught. A company gets its edge from the attitude of its people — its leaders, its supervisors, its front-line, back-office, entry-level, and long-term employees. Employees want to feel valued and appreciated and will most likely be more engaged and stay with an organization as a result. The higher the engagement level, the more their attitude barometer rises. The higher the attitude barometer rises, the more business will improve for an organization.

Building and maintaining healthy, effective relationships in all directions — with people you work for, people you work with, and people who work for you — is a key to success. Business is a team sport — that's a given. Nothing contributes more to the process of building effective work relationships than a positive attitude. More business successes are won on attitude rather than on technical achievement. A supervisor who demonstrates and knows how to build a positive attitude can lead a departmental workforce with only average experience and skills to achieve high productivity and successful performance. It's called "teamwork", and it happens often!

It's important to remember that we all have a choice — to be either positive or negative in any situation — and we make those choices every day. By keeping our power and being aware of our own attitude and choices, we can protect ourselves from external circumstances and the negativity of other people. Safeguard your attitude by solving personal conflicts quickly, taking the "high road" if someone behaves unreasonably or unfairly, insulating or distancing yourself from a person with whom you have a repeated conflict, focusing on the work, and changing your traffic pattern to avoid people who pull your attitude down. Remember: Your attitude belongs to you and to you alone! Here are some ways that you can use to help and foster and maintain positive attitudes in your workplace.

Set goals and deadlines: The greatest keys in helping people to become self-motivated are clear goals, a sense of purpose, urgency, and challenge. These elements provide a feeling of accomplishment, the

"Wow I did it!" feeling. People thrive on challenge and this will drive the positive attitudes in the workplace that you want.

Make sure you are motivated: It is impossible to help your team members have positive attitudes in the workplace if you are not positive. Instead of walking around and grumbling about the fact that people's attitudes aren't where you would like them to be, focus your energy on creating and finding the positive in others. Be a guiding light that lifts your people up. Encourage co-workers to achieve & create fulfillment in their work assignment: While not everyone working for you wants to be the next CEO of the company, most people do want more out of their jobs. Find out their goals, desires, and strengths and help them to create in their job more of that which causes them to feel fulfilled. Try to be flexible in your Leadership style: Emotional maturity and good judgment enable you to know when to be relaxed, open and warm to team members and when to put on the leader's hat, set limits and accept final responsibility.

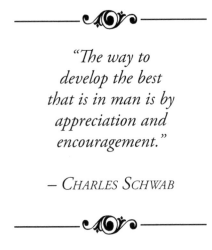

"The way to develop the best that is in man is by appreciation and encouragement."

— *CHARLES SCHWAB*

Listen to your team members opinions: There is a saying that the person closest to the task generally knows the best way of improving it. Tap into the knowledge and talent of your people. Help them to understand the 'real' constraints about why things may not always be able to be changed, but as best you can work to implement the suggestions they have to improve their job performance, quality of work or environment.

Promote respectfulness: Job titles may mean that there is a certain order to control and responsibility but that doesn't mean someone with a lesser job title is any less important. Respect each individual for what they bring to the organization. At the end of the day man would not have walked on the moon without the janitors making sure that the halls of NASA were pristine. Success and positive attitudes in the workplace are created when the entire team respects the value of each other's position and the diversity of thinking, talents, styles and experience each person brings.

Be appreciative of others: Ask anyone what is one of the biggest issues they have with their job and they are going to tell you that it is lack of recognition and appreciation. "What difference does it make if you do a good job or not, no one notices you until you mess up." Make an effort to let others know when they are doing a good job or not.

Show acts of kindness: This can be as little as offering a cup of coffee to someone who is feeling under the pump or giving a much-needed day off to someone who has gone above and beyond the call of duty. It will ensure others know that you care and that they are important to you.

Make work fun: Ok, so you can't throw a party at work every day. It is possible, though, to make the work day more fun. Fun can be a tool to help improve job performance and promote positive attitudes in the workplace. It doesn't have to be anything momentous - offering ice cream on a really hot day, a surprise lunch/morning tea, having a silly hat day. The effective use of humor can release stress of team members' creativity to resolve dilemmas because they feel safe to "think

"Enthusiasm is contagious. Be a carrier in the workplace."

– SUSAN RABIN

outside the box." The appropriate use of humor can create and maintain positive attitudes in the workplace.

Reward co-workers fairly: Many co-workers dislike their job position because of the pay. High wages do not motivate people, but low wages can bring about frustration, discouragement, and no motivation which causes bad attitude. So many organizations must make people feel they are fairly rewarded so that it is a non-issue for them. That will also enable them to have a positive attitude in the workplace.

Be open to new people, ideas, and processes that create positive changes and improved bottom-line results. The business world consists of many people who are different from you. We're dependent on each other to achieve common goals. We need to understand and work effectively with all our labor resources. Opportunities for us to learn about other generations, backgrounds, and cultures broaden our perspective and flourish us with new ideas, talents, and points of view — and it all affects bottom-line results!

A word of caution: Don't go overboard by becoming a noisy cheerleader who spends more effort on projecting your attitude than nurturing it. Above all, don't try to be someone you are not! Be who you are! Project the real thing! Be authentic!

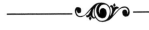

"Work is either fun or drudgery. It depends on your attitudes. I like fun."

— COLLEEN C. BARRETT

Life is a learning journey, and all we can do is continue to strive to do our very best each and every day. A wise person once said, "If you place more emphasis on keeping a positive attitude than on making money, you'll be successful and the money will take care of itself." Having a positive attitude in the workplace is not only important to how you do at work but also to how you do at home. Be good to yourself, enjoy the ride, and make a positive impact on your career and workplace with a positive attitude! Here are three positive tips that can help your co-workers to have a good attitude and work culture:

Appreciation: We must take time to appreciate our co-workers for the good job they have done or are doing. Let your co-workers know they have done great job.

Enthusiasm: Make it a point to display enthusiasm in everything you do. Having enthusiasm among your co-workers will help you get through the day quicker.

Have fun: The workplace is not just about work, for the simple reason that we are more than just machines. It is about people, interactions between them, and developing inter-personal relationships, as a team, have fun and foster a positive spirit; this keeps the "work train" chugging along — as it should.

We all want to feel good and enjoy our careers and our jobs in the workplace. But many of us have lost our way and no longer know how to find the joy in the everyday mundane tasks our jobs require. By cultivating a positive attitude in the workplace, you will slowly shift the energy and consciousness of the people around you. Just like some people can really bring you down, your attitude and behavior can elevate other people to greater heights and new possibilities.

*"By focusing
on improving
your attitude in
the workplace,
you will assume
a position of
leadership as you'll
quickly become an
influential source
of strength and
influence for those
around you."*

– JAMES M. KOUZES

CHAPTER 4

LEADERSHIP
IN THE WORKPLACE

Leadership is a valuable skill, especially in the workplace. The role of a leader or manager in the workplace is not easy because of his/her responsibilities, including: decision-making, planning, delegating, discipline and organizing. Some people seem to be born to lead, and others have to work at it. Whichever category you fall under, you can be sure that the ability to effectively lead others will improve your work environment and help you get the best out of your employees.

Everyone is not a leader to lead people, but everyone is a leader in the ability they offer in their workplace. The gift of leadership is a special ability to set goals for the future, and to explain these goals to others in such a way that they voluntarily and harmoniously work together to accomplish them. Traits for those with a gift of leadership include clear vision, the ability to focus on the greater goal of the group, and not obsessing over details.

Effective leadership begins from within. To successfully manage others, an individual must first learn how to manage him or herself.

A manager's initial priority should be to develop a **positive mental attitude**. Positive thinking reflects one's optimistic frame of mind. It means making the most out of everyday circumstances and looking at the bright side of things. Developing a more positive mental posture will uplift a person's spirits and improve an individual's outlook on life.

A real leader must always begin by being a servant first. When you understand how to be a servant, you understand the concept of serving people before taking on the role of a leadership position. I learn, as a leader, people will not follow you until they can see genuine interest in people's welfare.

"Good leaders must first become good servants."

-Robert Greenleaf

Obey them that have the rule over you, and submit yourselves: for they watch for your souls, as they that must give account, that they may do it with joy, and not with grief; for that is unprofitable for you (Hebrews 13:17).

The word "rule" means to lead or guide. That is why it is very important that associates respect and listen to their leaders because this is ordained by God. They are the ones who must give account before God; that is why being a leader in the workplace is very serious to God. An essential part of leadership or management is to influence the people you manage so that they do what you want them to do. The influence of a leader will depend on a variety of factors including the personality of them and those around them. For this purpose, we refer to those who are in leadership and management or leading as followers. The influence of a leader over his followers is often referred to as power.

Leadership is about influencing a group or team of people. It is not about power, titles and money although all these come with it but don't get the big head and forget about the purpose. Leadership is action-oriented. The vision is the articulation of the action to get to where the group needs to go. The vision should be well-defined and effectively communicated. Leaders believe that what they do is important and purposeful. The belief is the conviction that drives the leader's actions and passion. The conviction is communicated in the vision and nearly every statement of the leader. Leaders must have a purpose for their actions and what influences them. Leaders seek what is best for the group and not what is best for the

"Leadership is the capacity to influence others through inspiration motivated by passion, generated by vision, produced by a conviction, ignited by a purpose."

– DR. MYLES MONROE

individual. Leaders should be inherently selfless and hardworking. They are driven by their conviction and purpose and resonate the passion in their vision statements.

Leadership inspires and give hope, instead of instigating fear. They unite, not divide. A leader is a great communicator, surrounds him/her with the best advisers, and does not feel threatened by their capabilities.

After providing a vision and guidance, a leader does not interfere with his/her people's duties. A great leader always empowers, does what needs to be done, and doesn't get influenced by personal interest or short-lived public opinion. They are their own toughest critics.

They help their people to succeed, not oppress them. They coach, not reprimand. A great leader takes responsibility and does not use excuses or blame others for failures. They are visionaries and have purpose. They let ideas go free and enjoy watching them catch fire and become reality.

"A leader has the vision and conviction that a dream can be achieved. He inspires the power and energy to get it done."

– RALPH LAUREN

Some people are naturally drawn to leaders. The following are some of the characteristics that leaders commonly have. If these characteristics don't all come naturally to you, then make an effort to improve your weaker areas. Leadership skills can be developed through practice and experience. As a leader, you must establish principles concerning the way people (constituents, peers, colleagues, and customers alike) should be treated and the way goals should be pursued. Leaders must create standards of excellence and then set an example for others to follow.

LEADERS LEAD BY EXAMPLE

My father, on many occasions, told me that you do not command respect, you earn it. Whether you are in sales or another type of management, there are several principles you must understand to become a successful leader. The first is that you should never ask anyone to do anything you are not willing to do yourself. Many leaders in the workforce ask their employees to do things that may be unreasonable.

The best way to disprove that notion is to be ready to go out and do it yourself, if necessary. In such areas as these, you can gain or lose the respect of the people you lead every day. The best way to lead by example is for your employees to see you putting in extra hours when the workload is heavy, when there is a shortage of employees or be willing to listen to them. You can receive more respect from co-workers by putting in extra hours to accomplish a task or be willing to hear them out and see what they have to offer to the business or organization. The success of companies, large and small, in any organization is in the attitudes and behaviors of leaders of men and women. Leaders in an organization must, at all times, reflect an attitude of performance that they expect their employees to do. Leaders, you are obligated to make sure you provide the right tools and education for your employees to accomplish their tasks.

"A leader is one who knows the way, goes the way and shows the way."

– JOHN C. MAXWELL

As a leader, you must know that all situations are different. What you do in one situation will not always work in another. You must use your judgment to decide the best course of action and the leadership style needed for each situation. For example, you may need to confront an employee for inappropriate behavior, but if the confrontation is too late or too early, too harsh or too weak, then the results may prove ineffective.

VISIONARY LEADERSHIP

Visionary Leadership: Increase efficiency by moving decision-making responsibility to the frontline. Leadership must give co-workers the opportunity to develop the potential decision-making skills they have within themselves to better their workplace environment and the leader as well.

The Goal: The goal in any task is to get the job done. Leadership style controls efficiency, which controls the competitive value of products or services, which determines the winner. As a leader, you have to set goals, rules and regulations in your workplace and show no favoritism, be fair and firm.

Elementary problems: Leadership style controls the level of elementary problems which exist within the workplace. If there are any gaps in the workplace, you, as a leader, must find ways to fine-tune and bridge the gap. The level of elementary problems can be controlled, in part, by learning opportunities and a leader's personal priorities.

Leaders have direction: They are focused and have vision for their corporation or department, and they don't allow anyone or anything to distract them. Leaders work proactively, seeking new ideas and ways to improve things. They don't get bogged down with smaller problems, and they provide others with direction as well. When people see a good leader who follows through and is dedicated to the job, it inspires them to work hard and to be dedicated.

Effective leaders inspire and motivate others: They help others to see the importance of what they are doing and motivate them to do their best. A good leader understands that everyone works differently and takes note of others' preferred work methods. They are able to use this knowledge to get more out of their employees and co-workers and can show them that their contributions are important and valued.

Leaders are good communicators: They interact well with others despite the different personalities of employees they interact with, and they know how to confidently and effectively convey messages to others. In addition, effective leaders will usually make an effort to remember bits of personal information about others and will take note of their interests, skills, and experiences. Taking a personal interest in someone strengthens that person's working relationship and encourages them to be more dedicated.

Leaders are positive: They don't focus on the negative but inspire others by letting them see how important their contributions are. This doesn't mean that they never have any problems to deal with — they are human as well — but when they do, they do not get wrapped up in the negative; they look for the best solution and focus on reaching it by focusing more on the positive.

Successful leaders are solution driven: They don't allow co-workers to bring problems that cause division among them, but they can see problems and work for a solution, and they encourage others to help them and not stir up chaos. Leaders see the bigger picture and are constantly moving toward a specific goal.

Nobody is interested in following someone without a vision, most leaders has this ideal within themselves if I fit in and please everyone this will make me an exceptional leader. When you have no vision and no order you begin to neutralize your potential to be the leader you are called to be. When you are trying to lead, to fit in, or to make people like you, that is when you really start to lose your respect within the

"Dream lofty dreams, and as you dream, so shall you become. Your Vision is the promise of what you shall one day be. Your Ideal is the prophecy of what you shall at last unveil."

– JAMES ALLEN

workplace among your employees. Leaders must be different and they must stand up and they must have a vision for their workplace or business.

You cannot be a good leader without having a confidant, someone who you can trust and be open and honest with. Someone you can confide in about your frustration, stress and disappointment and you don't know what to do because you don't have the answers. You cannot be a great leader without having someone you can talk to and trust. Leaders must realize he or she will not have all the answers to solve the problems in workplace. That's why you need people who are with you and will stand by you in your good times and bad times. When you have a true confidant, you don't have to change your behavior they don't want you to be anyone else all they want from you "be you". Your confidant's commitment is to you, not to your causes. You are the center that causes the gravitation for your confidant to pull everything out of you to make you what you should be. A true confidant is not in it for the money, recognition, prestige or the title; they are in it for you. When you starve your confidant information about you in your life and you keep your emotion locked up within you and you refuse to tell your confidant, they will fall away and die emotionally. Any confidant you may have in your life, it's important to note that they move and breathe off of you. That is why your input is so vital to them, so they can help you to go to the next level. The greatness of leadership and productivity can only be found by resting in God and allowing Him to be in control and guiding you in the right path to take your business or organization to success.

"Without God, you can do nothing. With God, there is nothing you cannot do."

- CARSON KOLHOFF

LEADERSHIP PRODUCE LEADERS

We must understand that in every workplace there are hidden leaders that need to be revealed. There are many untapped leaders that need to be all that they can be and don't allow anything to hold them back. That is why the purpose of real leadership is to help train, develop and empower those who have that hidden potential to reach their destiny. This regulates true leadership and how leaders can invest and empower their followers to succeed in an organization.

"Leaders must understand they are only as good as their people"

— DAN RYAN

True leaders don't measure their success by how many people follow them, but they measure their success by how much they become unnecessary. True leadership is not measured in your presence, but in your absence. If your organization falls apart when you leave, you are not a leader. If the workplace doesn't know what to do in your absence, you are not a leader. Leadership is always measured in your absence because that shows how well you have produced leaders. This why it is very important to give those who have the potential to be the leader the empowerment, training and the skills to be ready when they are called upon.

"A leader…is like a shepherd. He stays behind the flock, letting the most nimble go out ahead, whereupon the others follow, not realizing that all along they are being directed from behind."

— NELSON MANDELA

MANAGEMENT VERSUS LEADERSHIP

It's important to understand the difference between leaders and managers. Managers are task-oriented. They supervise and direct workflow for maximum efficiency. Therefore, they tend to be more concerned about the process and the results, rather than about the employees and their individual needs. Leaders, on the other hand, are concerned not only about goals, but also about the people who are involved in the process. They must have a clear vision, must be able to effectively communicate that vision to others, and must have a strategy in mind for making that vision a reality.

Since communicating and implementing a vision will involve working with other people, true leaders are relationship-focused. They must inspire and motivate their followers, often playing the roles of coach and facilitator. When it comes to leadership, they know the weakness and power of their employees. When a leader has a good vision, they can read through people, those who are snowballing or con-artist in the workplace. They know those who are lazy and don't work as hard as others.

WHAT ARE THE TRAITS OF A DYNAMIC LEADER?

A dynamic leader not only possesses high moral standards, but also operates with a high sense of ethics and integrity, preferably for the good of the employees and the organization. Leaders take risks and understand the importance of change. They must have an appreciation of, and love for, learning. Does this mean that effective leaders never make mistakes? Absolutely not! While leaders do make mistakes, they use their mistakes as a learning tool, so that their chances of making the same mistake are nonexistent. Leadership is very important in the workplace today.

Effective leaders build a sense of communication and purpose within the workplace. They not only increase employee retention figures, but they also improve productivity because employees are more willing to follow effective leaders than non-effective individuals. Good leaders will give or bring in incentive treats that will improve the quality of the employee. True leaders of today must develop leadership skills. Leaders today, you must lead by experience, and speak from the heart at all times, which will cause your employees to see an effective leader is leading them. A good leader must know how to make good decisions under pressure. Leadership must realize that, in rapidly changing dangerous circumstances, decisions are made at times without thought. As a leader myself, I have heard and even uttered the words myself, "I didn't think about it. I just acted. We just did what had to be done".

"Decisions are at the heart of leader success, and at times there are critical moments when they can be difficult, perplexing, and nerve-racking"

— PROFESSOR HOSSEIN ARSHZSAM

LEADERSHIP MUST DISPLAY CERTAIN TRAITS

1. Integrity: Leaders have high ethics. They are honest. If you are to gain people's trust, then it is important to learn this trait early. Some of the actual situations where you can practice this behavior is taking responsibility for your own actions. Do not play the blame game when things go wrong. Leaders take personal responsibility for their team's actions and results.

2. Passionate: Leaders are passionate. They are enthusiastic about their work and they even have the ability to rub this energy off on their followers. Do you take on assignments given to you enthusiastically? This is one good behavior to start when developing leadership skills.

3. Commitment: When developing leadership skills, look at the easiest way to start. Commitment to your work is one of the easiest ways. Can you truly say you are willing to work hard at the job assigned? Leaders work hard and have a strong discipline in following through with their work.

4. Courageous: If people are to follow you, then, as a leader, you need to be courageous. Leaders are brave when they confront risks and the unknown. The ultimate test of a leader's courage is also the courage to be open. When looking at developing leadership skills, do you have the courage to speak up on things that matter?

5. Goal Oriented: Leaders are very focused on the objectives that need to be attained. They develop a plan and strategy to achieve the objectives. In addition, they will also need to build commitment from the team and rally them to achieve the organization's goal. When developing leadership skills, start by looking at how goal-oriented you are now. Improve upon that behavior.

6. Developing People: Developing people whether by training, coaching, or teaching them is one of the main traits of a good leader. No one can achieve organization goals alone. The team is needed in order to achieve them. Leaders develop the people to build a stronger team, so that the organization is effective. Start by developing your own knowledge when developing leadership skills.

7. Prioritize: Leaders do the most urgent and important things first regardless of their interest in them. For them, whatever needs to be done should be completed with the best possible effort. How do you fare with this trait? Do you do tasks that you are uncomfortable with?

Start developing leadership skills in this area by recognizing what are the important tasks to complete.

8. No Public Glory: Leaders understand that at best they will get private credit for their work. Public glory is not expected. They know whatever achievements are the result of joint effort of their units. They share glory and credit with the rest for the work.

They know they are only as good as their team. The team really is who knows and understands the daily job routines, so leaders need to listen and make sure their co-workers have all the tools they need to get the job done. When developing leadership skills, ask yourself this – are you generous enough to share the fruits of your unit's achievements? Developing leadership skills is a long process. Some people are born with such traits. They develop into leaders much faster. Leadership is also a set of behaviors as much as a skill. Hence, it is possible to learn leadership skills. Start now and when the opportunity arises, you will be ready.

BAD LEADERSHIP

There are many poor leaders in the workplace in many organizations that have no vision or goals. These leaders are in their particular positions only for power, titles, or money. Some leaders feel that the office or department is their kingdom and that they are the kings and queens in their organization. Bad leaders with negative self attitudes have a tendency to make an office or department look like hell on earth for their employees. Some leaders love to do things their way. Poor leadership has even caused stagnation within their workplace because some leaders are stubborn when they know something is not working. They always want to get their way, so they hurt the employees and make them look bad as the leader. They are highly individualistic, and they do not want to share the glory with employees at all! Not everyone in an executive leadership role is a good leader. Some leaders are bullies who abuse the power of their title or position simply because they can do so.

Some bullies are obvious – they throw things, slam doors, engage in angry tirades; they insult and are rude to their co-workers. Others, however, are much more subtle. While appearing to be acting reasonably and courteously on the surface, in reality, they are engaging in vicious and fabricated character assassinations, petty humiliations, and small interferences, any one of which might be insignificant in itself, but taken together over a period of time, they will poison the working environment. Many co-workers become afraid of their supervisor because of their negative, rude behavior, and attitude.

"If you want to be happy, set a goal that commands your thoughts, liberates your energy, and inspires your hopes."

– *ANDREW CARNEGIE*

As owners, bosses, directors, managers, supervisors, and pastors, never get a big head because of your position, and think you are all that, and you can treat your employees any kind of way. Because ultimately you are accountable before God and are the watchman over the employees. It is your duty and responsibility to do your job in the fear of God. When you treat people the wrong way, human resources may never know or find out, but always remember that God sees all and knows all. He will repay you for what you have done to His people (Romans 12:9). When all is said and done, everybody belongs to God, so be very careful what you say to them and how you handle them.

Many in management will attempt to threaten, intimidate,

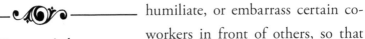

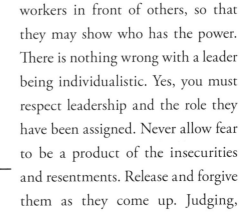

"Fear can't hurt you any more than a dream."

— WILLIAM GOLDING, LORD OF THE FLIES

humiliate, or embarrass certain co-workers in front of others, so that they may show who has the power. There is nothing wrong with a leader being individualistic. Yes, you must respect leadership and the role they have been assigned. Never allow fear to be a product of the insecurities and resentments. Release and forgive them as they come up. Judging, beating, or repressing insecurities just gives them power over you. Then you have a pattern that never gets resolved. Recognize that your real security is built from your relationship with your own heart. Will others look down on you? Some people might, but you can't control the thoughts or actions of other people, so why lose sleep over those who cause you to fear? But if you are in an organization, then you are connected to a team, where everyone is working together is imperative to the organization! Good leaders are *made* not born. If you have the desire and willpower, then you can become an effective leader. Good leaders are developed through a never-ending process of self-study, education, training, and experience.

FEARFUL WITHIN THE WORKPLACE

There are millions of people in the workplace around the world who are afraid of their boss, regardless of national culture. Fear can be dangerous. It can turn into a certain mindset in which the employees see the boss as a big, giant authority figure instead of as a leader.

Emotions play an important part in our daily lives. Fear is one such emotion that is pre-programmed into all animals and people as an instinctual response to potential danger. You cannot be scared of your boss if you want to be successful. You must respect them in their office. I am convinced that leaders must not abuse their power to make other people look small. Now, whether the fear is a product of the actions of your boss or a result of your own life experience, irrespective of who

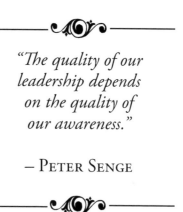

"The quality of our leadership depends on the quality of our awareness."

— Peter Senge

instills it, Dale Carnegie has argued that, "You can conquer almost any fear if you only make up your mind to do so. For remember, fear doesn't exist anywhere except in the mind".

Fear, as far as I can tell, is the result of uncertainty in a situation. We fear death because we do not know what happens after it. We fear losing our jobs because we don't know if there is another way we will be able to support ourselves. We fear asking a person out on a date because we don't know what the other person's expectations are and whether they would say yes or no. In all of these instances, fear comes from not knowing what we would do should a particular situation happen.

Change your attitude when it comes to fear of your boss or anyone else. Don't have the mindset that you are a failure because you didn't stand up to them. Most people fear failure for several reasons: Failure makes you a bad person, a loser that others look down upon; you could lose all or most of your money and/or your possessions. Both of these are misconceptions. Co-workers must realize that failure doesn't change your genes or your personality. It affects some people's actions negatively, but it is not negative in itself. A person becomes a failure or loser when they think they are a failure. It's not being down; it's staying down that makes you a failure. You can't control the thoughts or actions of other people, so why lose sleep over those who cause you to fear in your life?

The main point is that while it is true that failure can be uncomfortable and unpleasant, it is not life-threatening. Failure is always an opportunity of one kind or another — an opportunity to stretch beyond your accustomed boundaries and to learn something valuable. Remembering this positive face of failure will go a long way toward changing your attitude about your fear of anyone or anything. Here are a few ways you can deal with your boss without fear:

Initiate contact: Find ways to interact with your boss. It might be uncomfortable, but it's worth it. Keep your eyes on them. Make them feel that you are not afraid of them.

Be prepared: When speaking with your boss, you want to make sure that you have thought things through from every possible angle.

Humanize: Your boss is just like you — but with a bigger office and a fatter paycheck; don't lose sight of that. He or she could simply be having a bad day or having issues of their own. So, do not take their actions personally.

Disagree: Pick and choose your moments and know your audience. Keep in mind that good bosses do not want to be surrounded by "yes" people. Disagreeing on a small issue could help you prepare for a larger issue disagreement down the road.

Forgive yourself: Don't judge yourself too harshly if you stumble over a word or make a mistake. Instead, take measures to ensure success the next time around.

Overcoming fear on the job or with people is very important to maintain happy lifestyle. It is important to realize that in everything we do, there's always a chance that we'll fail. Facing that chance, and embracing it, is not only courageous – it also gives us a fuller, more rewarding life.

"Courage is never to let your actions be influenced by your fears."

-ARTHUR KOESTLER

CHALLENGES IN LEADERSHIP

In today's society in many business or organizations, many leaders are faced with personal images and challenges among their colleagues of likes and don't likes that always bring about confusion and disagreement. Many leaders are confronted by other leaders and co-workers who are out to sabotage them. So leaders must understand and realize that challenges and issues will arise from negative people who don't like you because they are full of drama. What many leaders don't realize is when negative people bring challenges and problems in their life, it's designed to take them to another level. Many people, who love to cause problems in your life, are either jealous or they just don't like you. Every leader must remain positive in a hostile environment, recognize the problems, learn from them, and then rise to the challenges of being an effective and true leader.

"Leaders would not be needed if there were no challenges in life."

- UNKNOWN

THE WORKPLACE WITHOUT ANY VISION

I am not talking about people without the ability of sight. I am talking about a manager or supervisor who has a company vision. Those in leadership who cannot see or even imagine the future of the company and/or their business or employees have no vision.

Where there is no vision, the people perish; but he that keepeth the law, happy is he (Proverbs 29:18).

When we come to read a text from the Bible, it is always good to see exactly what God is speaking to your spirit and what you should be listening to. *"Where there is no vision, the people perish."* In the first place, the word "vision" used here has to do with the Word of God. Where there is no message of life, the people perish. That is the primary interpretation of this passage. All effective managers and leaders must have vision. They must have the foresight and energy to direct the company or their place of business and its employees towards the prosperous goals. When the manager has vision and uses it in this manner, they create the energy that drives the productivity and their employees to excel. The employees feed off of that energy and it pushes them to go beyond the normal status quo. The vision is what sets the quest, the mission, and the charge that creates successful operations in the workplace to go to another level.

"What would be worse than being born blind?" She replied, "To have sight without vision." – Helen Keller

Too often in today's workplace, people are put into positions of leadership because they have paper certifications, who they know, buddy, buddy system or political associations. These same people who possess impressive resumes too often lack the vision to drive the mission for the company. It is simply this: Without a constant revelation of God's power and glory in and through us, we shall perish, and the world with us! God is simply reaffirming a basic tenet of faith — before anything great can ever be done, somebody has to catch a vision of it.

God says that any way other than His way is futile. In Ezekiel 7:15, He says that without Him, you'll only find a famine within and a sword without. Unless we see as God sees and understand as He would want us to understand, we will perish. I would like to point out three instances in the Bible when there was no vision or revelation from God.

"Give us clear vision that we may know where to stand and what to stand for-because unless we stand for something we shall fall for anything"

– *Peter Marshall*

Many times, because leaders in workplace have no vision of the physical future for company suffer, they keep going around in circles because they refuse to allow their vision to direct them in the way they should go.

Every vision is birth out of a burden, if you don't have burden for anything you have no vision. There comes heaviness within your soul that creates a vision that there is a need that has been birth in you to come forth. There are three components of vision:

- Hindsight: Understanding of a situation or event after it has happened; reflection.
- Insight: Seeing from within your business.
- Foresight: You cannot possess what you do not foresee.

Leonardo da Vinci, who painted the Last Supper, and Mona Lisa; he was an accomplished scientist, inventor, painter, sculptor, architect, musician, and writer. Leonardo da Vinci left in his studio notes of things that were going to be invented hundreds of years after his death.

When ask about the secret of his invention, he responded with his personal motto, which he called "Sapar Vedere". This phrase contains the Latin "Sapar", which means knowing how, and "Vadere", which means to see, so when you put them together it means "Knowing how to see". We, as leaders in the workplace, must learn to look beyond your dark clouds, storms in your life and have faith in God's Word to help strengthen your place of work. The leaders must lead the vision and be deeply involved in the process from beginning to end by heralding the vision weekly to their employees. Building or articulating a vision is a spiritual task and sometimes become difficult because no vision casting in the workplace is worth the paper it is printed on, unless it is generated by prayer, consistence and characterized by faith (Hebrews 11:1). One of the key tasks is communicating the vision in appealing ways. After the vision statement has been written, it should be reduced to a memorable slogan that can be easily remembered. A commercial designer or artist can be used to develop an attractive visual representation of the vision slogan.

"It is one thing to have a vision, but without clear communication, vision will never come to pass."

- Unknown Quote

UNDERCOVER BOSS

Have you ever see the show on TV called Undercover Boss? Every week, the CEO of a different large or small enterprise puts on a disguise and "goes undercover" to learn what employees really think, and what challenges they face-at work and in life. Inevitably, the undercover boss is remarkably at executing the more granular, foundational-tasks on which their organizations run-and walks away with a healthy new respect for challenges that are faced by employees every day.

Many leaders don't even know what goes on in the workplace because either they are too busy or they don't even care. As a leader you must has hands on experience, get involved with the workload, when problems arise among your employees than you will know how to solve the problems before they escalate. So what's so intriguing about watching CEOs and leaders do the jobs that so many of us do on a daily basis? Will this be fun watching them struggle to stock shelves or etc… or will this make you feel I glad to see them learning hand experience and see how this workplace can be improved.

Think about your organization as a leader by considering doing work not in a suit or in a dress, doing things you don't normally do, so that you can gain a different perspective and a greater respect among your employees. While working alongside their employees, they will see the effects their decisions have on others, where the problems lie within their organization and gets an up-close look at both the good and bad while discovering the unsung heroes who make their company succeed in its everyday operations.

> *"Great leaders today are masters of persuasion. They can effectively communicate ideas and build support and buy-in largely because they are able to 'connect' with others. Emotional maturity and approachability make them well-liked, respected, and therefore effective."*
>
> — LAUREN ELWARD, CEO, CASTLE INK, AN INK CARTRIDGE SUPPLIER

MANAGEMENT SHOULD BE HELD RESPONSIBLE

Managers and supervisors must give accountability for their actions. If leaders are not held accountable for employee motivation and actions, then the employees are lacking direction and may be left to flounder. Many managers reach their positions through natural progression up the corporate ladder. They get where they are based on the strength of their abilities and strength. The most important thing to remember is that most of them never had any training in managing people. They may be the best at what they do, but if they can't get the best out of their people, then productivity will suffer, as will profitability.

As leaders in workplace, always be open-minded, and glean from your employees. Sometimes, it is good to have a suggestion box, and give your employees incentives. Make them feel appreciated for what they do for the company. Effective managers are those who focus on learning and utilizing management techniques that lead to increased productivity, effectiveness, efficiency, customer satisfaction, and employee development. Some of the more effective management techniques that have been identified include the use of change agent skills, coaching, monitoring employee performance, accountability, and the ability to motivate.

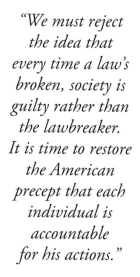

"We must reject the idea that every time a law's broken, society is guilty rather than the lawbreaker. It is time to restore the American precept that each individual is accountable for his actions."

— Ronald Reagan

Accountability influences job commitment and satisfaction of employees, which will cause a good atmosphere of teamwork. In order for employees to consistently perform at their best, it is important that managers provide a clear statement as to what is expected and to what standards from their employees.

It also needs to be clear to employees that they will be held accountable for ensuring that these expectations and standards are met. However, of equal importance, managers must be willing to demonstrate accountability for their own performance. Employees perform at their best when accountability is evident and they have managers who live up to standards of sincerity and integrity within the workplace.

WHAT MAKES A GREAT LEADER?

Here are ten vital traits a great leader should have. Over the years, many people have talked and written about what makes a great leader. They have derived examples from some of the greatest public and private figures in both the past and the present. Good leadership is putting God first, know and understand your purpose and vision and how to work with your co-workers as a team.

To help you improve your own leadership skills, here are ten good examples of what makes a great leader.

1) Determination

A great leader has an almost inexhaustible stock of determination. He is the first one to initiate an idea and the last one to give up. It is because of a leader's determination that projects are completed.

2) Flexibility

What makes a leader great? It is his ability to adapt to any situation. He sees the situation from many different angles and can adjust himself accordingly.

3) Resourcefulness

Sometimes, not everything is handed to you on a silver platter. No one was born with a silver spoon in their mouth; they have to work hard for it. In these cases, you're going to have to think of other ways to get what you want, or to achieve what you want to achieve. Coupled with flexibility, resourcefulness is definitely a powerful leadership tool.

4) Creativity

Another vital factor on what makes a great leader is his creativity. Creativity is not just about art and aesthetics. It is also about being able to solve a problem with the least amount of time, money, and effort.

5) Self-confidence

Without self-confidence, how can a leader expect to get his people to follow him? But keep in mind that self-confidence is different from arrogance. Don't make the mistake of confusing one for the other, or you'll soon find yourself being the target of everybody's ire.

6) Positive Attitude

A great leader has a positive countenance but is not overtly idealistic. Instead, he tries to make the best out of everything.

7) Responsibility

Responsibility is a double-edged sword. A great leader understands that whatever happens in his team (whether good or bad) is his responsibility. He does not hog all the glory and does not play the blame game with his subordinates. If the program or project fails, he takes the blame as well.

8) Good Communication Skills

Never underestimate the power of good communication skills. As a leader, you will be tasked to oversee everything that comes and goes.

What makes a leader great is his ability to communicate effectively with his team. A good leader understands that people don't perceive messages in the exact same way.

9) Consistency

How credible, do you think, is a person who only does well during certain months? A great leader is a fine example of consistency. He takes actions and delivers, project after project.

10) Forecasting

A good leader knows what's up ahead. He has the ability to estimate the projected value of a certain object in the future. So what makes a great leader? It is a mix of these qualities. You don't necessarily have to possess all of them, but you should at least strive to develop many of them.

As a leader, you need to interact with your followers, peers, seniors, and others; whose support you need in order to accomplish your goals. To gain their support, you must be able to understand and motivate them. To understand and motivate people, you must know human nature. Human nature is the common qualities of all human beings. People behave according to certain principles of human nature. As a leader, you must understand these needs because they can be powerful motivators to you in leadership.

This is common sense. If you want to lead, you need to have a vision to show others where you are going. Still, it is amazing how many organizations suffer because their leaders don't cast a clear vision.

*"Lead and inspire
people. Don't try
to manage and
manipulate people.
Inventories can
be managed but
people must be
lead".*

– ROSS PEROT

CHAPTER 5

CLIQUES IN THE WORKPLACE

I must admit that the workplace is not an appropriate setting for cliques or rather individual socializations. This is because clubs within a workplace can produce negative connotations. Cliques do very little to inspire the spirit of camaraderie. All employees must advocate team playing by supporting team building, not separatism. What are the pros and cons of cliques in the workplace? Webster defines a "clique" as a narrowly exclusive group of people usually held together by a common, "often selfish", interest or purpose. Since individuals have different mindsets, it's possible that there may be arguments or differences of opinion regarding certain issues. You'll find this kind of attitude happening most often in places of work.

Usually there are cliques that cause the most intense conflicts within the environment of the workplace. Oftentimes, cliques are very rude, thoughtless, self-centered, and arrogant when relating to people who are not a part of their group. At the workplace, there are no guarantees that you will be liked by everyone, because it's a place where you spend time where there are people who will like and won't like you. Cliques in the workplace will engage in hearty arguments, and they will cause hurt feelings and disappointments as well, because cliques in the workplace have no rules. No matter what job you have, you may find employees who love to keep up a mess as a group. In most instances, a clique starts out as people who form close friendships and then begin to start alliances to make it easy on themselves, or to make it hard on others.

Some co-workers in the workplace have a toxic, bad attitude, which is a form of mental abuse, and makes their presence uncomfortable for their fellow co-workers. When those co-workers with toxic behavior are on sick leave, or on vacation, many of the co-workers feel like it is an annual holiday. Dealing with difficult people is much tougher when they are attacking you or undermining your professional contribution in the workplace.

Sometimes, cliques get out of hand, hurting people in the workplace because they refuse to agree with their negative agenda, or they simply turn into a hateful group of people who find strength in numbers and target other employees with their negative attitudes. People who love to run in cliques can be very childish in manner, mean-spirited, and intimidating to other employees.

"Every clique is a refuge for incompetence. It fosters corruption and disloyalty; it begets cowardice, and consequently is a burden upon and a drawback to the progress of the country. Its instincts and actions are those of the pack."

– MADAME CHIANG KAI-SHEK

This causes stress and discontent in the workplace, as there is division.

Many cliques develop favoritism and politics because of someone or something they don't agree with. Cliques are like spoiled children; they get mad if they can't have their way. It is unwise to try and force your way into a clique, because it can lead to hurt feelings in others and disappointments. There are no rules which say that cliques have to accept you.

Cliques are a deadly attitude in the workforce. They are out to destroy someone's reputation. Where there are a few or more negative people in a group, there is something stirring in their minds. When cliques hear something negative, they begin to spread negative information to make themselves feel good.

Many co-workers spread gossip among their certain cliques, which brings about division and frustration in the workplace. Many employees spread gossip in huddles in their groups during their breaks, because they want to rip a person's reputation down. Cliques bring about jealousy, contentions, backbiting, and spreading rumors about others. What many cliques fail to remember is when you gossip about others, then those in your clique will one day turn on you and begin to gossip about you behind your back.

GROUPS AND CLIQUES CAUSES DIVISION IN THE WORKPLACE

There are many evil groups that have formed cliques that have caused much division and pain in their workplace. Most cliques will always follow a weak-minded person in the workplace because they feel if they follow the crowd, they will succeed in group. There are the boss and supervisor, who also hang out in cliques with their employees because of favoritism. Then there are so many co-workers in the workplace, who love to be a part of groups to tear other people's reputations down. Those who are apart of groups or cliques feel that they are better or superior to other people because they are a part of this certain group. Those who are affiliated with a group or cliques are hypocrites, and they will laugh in your face with a false perception and put on a façade. Some people in the workplace love to put on a façade, which differentiates from the real person.

Groups can be a positive or negative component in the workplace. When groups or teams work together, they will accomplish so much. On the other hand, those negative groups always cause gossip, spread rumors, and cause division in workplace.

Focusing on the positive as a group

- Groups have the empowerment to work as a team.
- Groups will pitch in and get the job done.
- Groups will create a happy environment.
- Groups understand they can work any department to accomplish certain task.

Focusing on the negative as a group

- Groups will alienate themselves from others.
- Groups are close minded people.
- Groups will only bring about chaos.
- Groups are bullies.

Preventing the formation of negative groups in the first place is the preferred course of action. Encourage open communication and conflict resolution among all your staff. Be upfront about how you want everyone to resolve even minor disagreements among one another early on, instead of prolonging the dispute or going to others for coalition-building. Consider providing training on communication or conflict resolution as a way to demonstrate your support for early intervention.

In the workplace, co-workers must develop respect for each other and forget about groups and cliques and work as a team. When you work as a team, you share responsibility and you delegate the tasks to help develop the skills in each other. Challenge the team so they are given opportunities to grow and stretch. This means they may make mistakes – make sure they know that's okay and help them to learn and recover from them. A formal team is a structured team, created for a specific purpose. It will have a leader and everybody within the team will have a distinct role.

*"We can work together
but we can't just work
with each other."*

- AULIQ ICE

CLIQUES BRINGS ABOUT GOSSIP IN WORKPLACE

There is a deadly spirit of gossip that is caused when a group of employees, with negative attitudes, get together and begin to get in their huddle to slander and destroy a person's reputation. Many co-workers today are caught up in cliques or groups that are only out to slander and spread rumors about others. When you become a part of an allegiance or clique in the workplace, you are setting your own self up to have a bad reputation. By their very definition, cliques are exclusive, leaving others on the outside. Webster's defines a clique as a small group of people, with shared interests or other features in common, who spend time together and do not readily allow others to join. Many cliques will go and spread rumors and say, "You didn't hear this from me, but mum's the word". We found out that men love to gossip about other in the workplace because they love to criticize another person's behavior. People who are in cliques will spread bad rumors about someone, and they will tell others. The legendary song writer, Marvin Gaye, famously declared that he "heard it through the grapevine". Gossip is the kind of thing that's titillating to hear and fun to participate in…unless you're the subject of the latest workplace tittle-tattle.

Bad cliques exclude anyone from joining, and they really have nothing to do with friendship. Once formed around negativity, members frequently engage in petty and disruptive gossip. At their best, members' uncooperativeness and narrow-mindedness cause great amounts of grief for others around them; at their worst, members may even bully co-workers who do not belong. There are people trying to fit in, so they will get involved with certain clicks and they will begin to gossip, lie and do what it takes to stay in the cliques in workplace. The phrase, "Birds of a feather flock together" means that people who are similar to each other spend time together. They can identify with each other because they have the same spirit.

There are so many employer and employees who are a part of an organization who are connected to some form of cliques in their workplace. These people bring about division, confusion, wounds and chaos in our Country, workplace, community and local churches. Many co-workers spread gossip in their so-called cliques because they can't stand a person and they want to see that individual's reputation ripped apart. Some employee will only associate with certain co-workers within their office or place of business because they want certain people to quit or join our cliques. The real issues of cliques they have a jealous attitude.

"There will always be a few people who just want to knock you down or are jealous or just want to be horrible for the sake of it. I don't know what drives someone to be nasty."

-GERI HALLIWELL

CONFLICT THAT ARISES IN BUSSINESS MEETINGS

In many businesses meeting today in workplace, they call a monthly or yearly meeting or a special meeting that sometimes devolves into disagreements, division or hatred. Many workplaces have meetings because they want to inform their associate or to resolve certain issues. I have seen some department meetings start with animosity and end up in division. No business or department should be divided, but we must speak the same thing (1 Corinthians 1:10). I have seen so many business and workplace torn apart by unresolved conflicts or small issues that they heard in meetings and they got upset and took something that was said and blew it out of proportion.

There have been tension and debates in meetings that have caused anger and mad at one another. This can be exciting and energizing, but it can also hurt the team's progress and morale. If you're in charge of a meeting and conflict occurs, what is your role? How do you restore peace? How can you assure that these conflicts don't harm your work?

Can it be saved based on the teams' morale? Here are a few key pointer a those who help facilitator or to help improve dysfunctional meeting because of people negative attitudes.

. Have a plan
. Have a set time
. Have an agenda
. Have a basic topic
. Have handouts
. Have input
. Have meeting always under control
. Have meeting adjourned.

Sometime in meeting, there are going to be conflicts. Many will give off sigs such as whispering, writing and passing notes and give off body language. I have seen from experience that conflicts can be very disruptive. But I have also notice that if we fail not to deal with our conflict we have fail to communicate. Many times by talking about conflicts in a business meeting will cause the group to help solve and work on a solution to the problem. Regardless of the type of conflict you are dealing with, listen to everyone opinion to help solve the department. To become a good conflict manager requires a lot of practice. Just remember that the goal is to reach a compromise that both of you can live with as well as be happy with. In other words, find a way that both of you can walk away feeling like a winner!

*"A true leader has the
confidence to stand alone,
the courage to make
tough decisions, and the
compassion to listen to the
needs of others. He does
not set out to be a leader,
but becomes one by the
equality of his actions and
the integrity of his intent."*

— DOUGLAS MACARTHUR

CLIQUES USE BODY LANGUAGE

Workplace body language can change how you are perceived at work. Body language nonverbally communicates what a person wants to say or do. We know that smiling is considered a form of welcome in many cultures, but it may also be perceived as a form of embarrassment to some. Many cliques that don't agree with someone or don't like someone, go on the defensive by rolling their eyes, pointing their fingers, turning their heads, and refusing to listen to you. They are really saying to you, "I'd rather you were not here", as simple as that.

Body language is a very important aspect when communication with others at the workplace. Most of your communication is done by body language. If your body (mind) has a good attitude, then your body language will be good in the workplace. Some cliques within the workplace model poor body language; because they use it as a weapon to say what they really have no courage to say to the person.

When you walk into a room filled with people, your body language will project positive energy or negative energy. With the positive, you will attract people, but with the negative, you will tell others that you don't want to be around them, don't like them, or won't allow them to think negative thoughts about you. Now I think you can answer your own question: what benefits you will you have with positive energy vs. negative energy? Body language is about the signals you send out to others, and these signals will influence how they "see" you. So, understanding body language can maximize the first impression people have of you. Most folks make a decision about another within 30 seconds of meeting them. Bad body language makes you feel unwanted and uninteresting, whereas, good body language makes people feel valued, wanted, and that they are worth spending time with and conversing with.

Don't be afraid to get in touch with your feminine side when you are communicating with your co-workers. Learn to be persistent and to get through to your co-workers, whether it's through body language or communicating with words, your main goal is to get them to open up. I believe that face-to-face communication is better than any other form of communication, because if you want to talk to someone about some important matters, you should talk in person so that you can understand each other.

"The nice thing about teamwork is that you always have others on your side."

— MARGARET CARTY

Communicating in person helps share both verbal and body posture information as it gives a chance to read someone's gestures when communicating with them. Make your co-worker feel good about himself by using effective communication.

LAZY PEOPLE IN THE WORKPLACE

In every workplace, there is always that one person who doesn't pull his weight. He will come in late, leaves early and spends the day chatting, sitting down, taking extra-long breaks, having personal phone calls, walking around the office and bothering people. Everyone in the workplace has discerned his slacker behavior, but the fact that he keeps engaging in it makes you mad and frustrated. "Some [slackers] are not aware [of their behavior]; they may have a perpetual victim mentality and feel justified, or will find an excuse or reason for their behavior," says Mark Goulston, author of *Just Listen*. However, many are aware and just don't care enough to try harder to pitch in to help their team out. The main reason they continue with the behavior and are lazy is because they know their bosses and employees won't say anything and refuse to hold them accountable. So, many boos, supervisor and co-workers realize that certain employees are lazy, but they choose to ignore this behavior because they want to avoid confrontation.

The French author Jules Renard once wrote, "Laziness is nothing more than the habit of resting before you get tired". The comic strip Blondie once had Dagwood Bumstead offer this bit of humorous wisdom about laziness, "You can't teach people to be lazy - either they have it, or they don't." Laziness, as it relates to employers and employees, is the gross failure to have the heart of your company and team that will perfect one mind, and to serve your customer effectively. It is the tendency to do nothing in the face of opportunity. Laziness, a lifestyle for some, is a temptation for all. But the Bible is clear that, because the Lord ordained work for man, laziness is sin. *Go to the ant, you sluggard! Consider her ways and be wise* (Proverbs 6:6). Laziness is also the failure of a person to properly manage their time and resources while they are on the job. I have found out, in my years of working with people, there are people who are very lazy in the workplace. Working with a lazy colleague can be a challenging and discouraging experience. Lazy co-workers, who don't work to the best of their ability, can damage the morale of the entire team, and even cause negative repercussions in the workplace. Usually, your first step to solve the problem will be to meet with your colleague in private. Yes, he will be defensive and say "I work and I do my share", but you have to let him know how his poor performance is impacting your own work and the team. You can also try to help him by subtly changing his motivation and behavior attitude. If, however, this approach doesn't work after you've given him several chances to improve, you'll need to hand the problem over to your boss. It's their responsibility to handle staff issues, once you've done all that you can. As a co-worker, do your job well and don't be distracted or obsessed by those who are slackers or lazy in workplace. If you do your work well, it will shine; others will notice. Work well and stay focused while working with lazy co-workers because they lower their standard in the workplace. As a servant of God in the workplace, remember that He sees all and He knows who works and who doesn't work.

*"A life of leisure and a life
of laziness are two things.
There will be sleeping
enough in the grave."*

-*Benjamin Franklin*

TEAMWORK IN THE WORKPLACE

The approach, which we as co-workers must take to achieve a lean operation, is team-based. So, being "lean" is about the reduction of certain attitudes and behaviors which keep us from working as a team. Have you ever been working on a project alone and you wanted to do it all by yourself, so you could get all the credit. This kind of attitude really makes you look bad. Teamwork is defined as an activity or a set of inter-related activities in the workplace. Michael Jackson wrote song "We are one"; he believed that all humans are unique and equal, regardless of race or culture, and that working together as one will make for a better world. His message was one of unity, harmony and hope.

"Unity is strength…when there is teamwork and collaboration, wonderful things can be achieved."

-MATTIE STEPANEK

You should have a tightly knit team amongst co-workers who care deeply about each other and the well-being of the department, organization, or the customers. Managers and employees should bear in mind that no man is an island. At your workplace, having a team that works for a common vision is the greatest advantage. When co-workers work as a team, they can actually get the job done quicker and in a more efficient way. When people are willing to work as a team, they are willing to come together. Teamwork is essential to the vitality and the life of the workplace. One person cannot do it all. Trying to do everything is not an effective method in the workplace as a team.

Michael Jordan, the famous basketball player for the Chicago Bulls, knew that although he was a great player, he could not win by himself. Michael knew it took teamwork to be effective. Michael's acknowledgement that he needed help made him even more effective on the court, and, season after season, the Chicago Bulls won championship after championship. Why; because of effective teamwork. Michael may have been the star player on the team and even the centerpiece in some people's eyes; however, Michael understood that in order to be effective, you can't be afraid to get in touch with your softer side that will cause you to lay down your pride and get others involved as a team.

> *"A group becomes a team when each member is sure enough of himself and his contribution to praise the skills of the others."*
>
> *– NORMAN SHIDLE*

Be persistent! Communicate face-to-face! Mirror body language! Make people feel good about themselves! Move forward! Strive! Be courageous! Enjoy the hope of life and the indomitable will you have been given! Don't hesitate — act! When a team begins to share the same passion and focus to achieve the desired goal, then it will make them feel as though they are responsible for the outcome and this strengthens the bond between co-workers.

OVERCOMING CLIQUES

Whenever there are groups of people, cliques have an opportunity to form. These are closed groups of people, clubs of exclusive members.

Such groups can defeat any attempt to form a companywide atmosphere of teamwork. It is not a good idea to try and break up a clique. It would be better for the clique in question to be given a role as a group and work with a person of expertise. When dealing with difficult co-worker in workplace you will be faced with all sorts of dysfunctional approached to deal with negative co-workers. Placing a note of kindness is not an option. Confronting the bullies or cliques can often lead to disaster. Telling the boss will not be a good move as well. So, let's look at more productive ways to address your difficult co-worker.

These are five productive ways to deal with your difficult co-worker and cliques in workplace.

Start out by examining yourself. Are you sure that the other person is really the problem and that you're not overreacting? Always start with self-examination to determine that the object of your attention really is a difficult person's actions and nit your own perception.

"In order for co-workers to be effective they must learn how to stay in their own lane."

— RYAN D. ISOM

Explore what you are experiencing with a trusted friend or colleague. Brainstorm ways to address the situation. When you are attacked, or your boss appears to be supporting the dysfunctional actions of a co-worker, it is often difficult to objectively assess your options. Pay attention to the unspoken agreement you create when you solicit another's assistance. You are committing to act unless you agree actions will only hurt the situation. Otherwise, you risk becoming a whiner or complainer in the eyes of your colleague.

Approach the person with whom you are having the problem for a private discussion. Talk to the co-worker about what you are experiencing in "I" messages. (Using "I" messages is a communication approach that focuses on your experience of the situation rather than on attacking or accusing the other person.) You can also explain to your co-worker the impact of their actions on you. Be pleasant and agreeable as you talk with the other person. They may not be aware of the impact of their words or actions on you. They m know their impact on you and deny it or try to explain it away. Unfortunately, some difficult people just don't care; especially during a discussion when attempts to reach an agreement about positive and supportive actions going forward.

Follow up after the initial discussion. Has the behavior changed? Gotten better? Worse? Determine whether a follow-up discussion is needed. Determine whether a follow-up discussion will have any impact. Decide if you want to continue to confront the difficult person by yourself. Become a peacemaker. Determine whether you have experienced a pattern of support from your boss.) If you answer, "yes," to these questions, hold another discussion. If not, escalate and move to the next idea.

You can confront your difficult co-worker's behavior publicly. Deal with the person with gentle humor or slight sarcasm. Or, make an exaggerated physical gesture – no, not that one – such as a salute or place your hand over your heart to indicate a serious wounding. You can also tell the difficult person that you'd like them to consider important history in their decision making or similar words

"Try to have as diverse group of friends as possible and don't get into the clique scenario."

– Andrew Shue

expressed positively, depending on the subject. Direct confrontation does work well for some people in some situations. I don't think it works to ask the person to stop doing what they're doing, publicly, but you can employ more positive confrontational tactics. Their success for you will depend on your ability to pull them off. Each of us is not spur-of-the-moment funny, but if you are, you can use the humor well with difficult co-workers.

Recognize that the only thing you as a co-worker are truly in charge of is how you choose to react to cliques and difficult co-workers in any situation. I trust that these ideas will help you in addressing the negativity in your workplace that will cause you to be honest, trustworthy and bring about teamwork in workplace.

TOO MANY CHIEFS, NOT ENOUGH INDIANS

There is an expression you should familiarize yourself with: "In order to be a general, you have to be a good solider first." What this

"Talent wins games, but teamwork and intelligence wins championships."

— *MICHAEL JORDAN*

means is that you need to work your way up and learn from those above you. In many organizations, there are co-workers who want to be in the leadership positions but never want to be a servant among the people. There are too many co-workers trying to be in charge and telling others what to do, but there are not enough workers to do the work. Some people in the workforce want to have power over others, but nothing is getting done because everyone is bossing or directing, and there is no one taking directions and following them through. In many workplaces, there is a great need for "Indians" who will be responsible for the workload, and they should have a servant attitude to build teamwork. True "Indian" co-workers will not step on each other's toes or override management.

In the workplace, co-workers must share the vision by creating a great teamwork culture; a common vision is essential. "Without vision, the people perish," the Bible famously says. A vision is essential to an organization. It is a group of people headed by someone or by another group of people. The greatest challenge an organization can have is working together and sharing the same vision. Sometimes a vision is birthed and articulated by a single person. Sometimes it is a group sentiment.

A lack of vision will gradually destroy an organization or seriously disable it. Competing visions can also seriously fracture an organization. Eventually, a big picture vision has to prevail. My thesis is that cliques at work have some helpful components, but they often do more harm than good by being exclusive elements in the culture. Top performance in any organization requires the best effort of the entire team, and when parts of the group are fragmented into insular cells, all kinds of gremlins creep into the structure. In the extreme, cliques can be hurtful to the mission of an organization. But cliques are as natural as pancakes for breakfast. They form spontaneously and have their own unwritten by-laws that serve the members very well.

"If you want to make peace with your enemy, you have to work with your enemy. Then he becomes your partner."

— NELSON MANDELA

Cliques in the workplace can be demoralizing, but you can turn the situation around. By understanding the issues that face your workplace and taking positive action, you can help solve the problem and make your workplace a place where you really want to be at with people you want to be around as a team that will causes your co-workers to strive for teamwork and success.

CHAPTER 6

CONFLICTS
IN THE WORKPLACE

In our environment, we meet different people, and each of them has their own potential and weaknesses. We interact with them in different ways. However, we cannot please everyone by being who we are, and, thus, during these instances, conflicts might arise. Conflicts are normal for those people who are misunderstood and for those who will misunderstand the attitude of somebody else. Conflicts commonly happen in the place where we are working because we cannot deny the fact that competition among the employees is still there, especially when someone is craving a promotion. The diverse values and beliefs that we share may cause conflict. There are common conflicts that you can certainly face when you are at work, and one of these is the interdependence conflict.

Conflicts arise from a clash of perceptions, goals, or values in the arena where people care about the outcome. Where there are people, there are bound to be disagreements, misunderstandings, and ego clashes, all leading to conflicts. The breeding ground for conflict may lie in confusion about, or disagreement with, or misunderstanding of the common purpose and how to achieve it while also achieving individual goals within an organization.

When there is negative competition, internal and external attitudes will bring about conflicts among co-workers. There are all types of problems that exist in the workplace environment, from who is getting paid the most, problems with titles, positions, who is working or not working, break times, workloads, who is lazy, and many other conditions that can create unease among employees. Workplace conflicts among co-workers can be a cause or product of stress in the work environment. These conflicts should not be ignored, as they may eventually lead to fracturing within an organization and should be dealt with swiftly.

"The better able team members are to engage, speak, listen, hear, interpret, and respond constructively, the more likely their teams are to leverage conflict rather than be leveled by it."

— *RUNDE AND FLANAGAN*

Most conflicts in the workplace can be resolved by just reaching out to the other person and communicating frankly and tactfully. Yelling or howling at him or her is not at all advised; instead, calmly state facts and make them realize how his or her behavior is adversely affecting your work. Make them realize that you are a team, that you do not want this to boil into a full-scale conflict, and that you both are in the same boat and be open when you are not pleased about something.

There is so much conflict within the workforce today. Many co-workers feel as if "they have better things to do with their time than baby-sit with a bunch of feuding children". This type of attitude is called conflict; it is a normal and natural part of the workplace and of a person's life. Conflicts can be helpful in making necessary changes within the home or work environment. However, unresolved conflicts can result in hurt feelings, dissatisfaction, unhappiness, hopelessness, depression, and other emotions. It can result in behaviors, such as physical or emotional withdrawal, resignation from jobs, dissolution of personal relations, aggressions, or even violence.

Conflict is inevitable in the workforce today. It's not a matter of *whether* it will happen, but *when* it will happen. Employees are sometimes involved in conflict situations which may lead to the regrettable consequences of animosity, disagreements, and unforgiving attitudes that cause division within the workplace. We defined conflict as: "a state of discord caused by the actual or perceived opposition of needs, or a battle, disagreement between two or more parties."

"Man must evolve from all human conflict through a method which rejects revenge, aggression and retaliation. The foundation of such a method is love."

— MARTIN LUTHER KING, JR.

Unity is one of the crucial factors for having an effective team within the workforce. Conflict often comes to threaten unity among co-workers. How does one respond to conflict? This is a question that many leaders and born again believers desire to know. Problem solving within the workplace is very critical to the environment of the workplace. When faced with problems, people tend to be afraid or uncomfortable and wish it would go away. The person might even leave the workplace for good. When there are conflicts in the workplace, they feel that they have to come up with an answer, and it has to be the right answer, and they look for someone to blame. Being faced with a problem — becomes a problem. Conflicts can create an atmosphere among co-workers that causes stress in the work environment and disarray.

Many bosses, managers, and supervisors are master "avoiders" when it comes to conflict. They see conflict as a threat in the workplace environment or to relationships among other co-workers, but they fail to deal with it because of the person's attitude. What they fail to realize is that avoiding conflict leads to serious consequences, which actually endanger the workplace or someone's relationships instead of preserving them. There is a Chinese proverb that says:

Avoidance is very common and is employed when the individual withdraws, avoids, suppresses, and denies the existence of conflict. This action — or more appropriately, inaction — will typically cause the conflict to resurface at some point in the future in a more dramatic or adversarial form. When people avoided conflict because they think it has gone away — it is simply being postponed.

"People respond better to kindness than cruelty. Why, it's even caught on in the workplace, that bastion of self-hatred and disrespect."

– CHERI HUBER, AUTHOR

CONFLICTS AND DISPUTES IN WORKPLACE

Conflicts at work take many forms. It might be an individual with a grievance, a problem between an employee and a manager, or conflict between two co-workers. Any conflict can get in the way of work and make your business less productive. Dealing with conflict and disputes at an early stage to nip it in the bud and stop the situation from developing into a full-blown dispute will save time, money and stress later on, for both the employer and employees. In the workplace every day, disputes and conflicts of all types occurs in workplaces. The conflicts that arise in workplaces may be shaped by the unique aspects of this environment, including the long hours many people spend at their workplace. The causes of disputes and conflicts in the workplace can be tied to misunderstanding (communication failure), personality clashes, value and goal differences, substandard performance, differences over method, responsibility issues, lack of cooperation, authority issues, frustration and irritability, competition for limited resources, and non-compliance with rules and policies. All types of disputes and conflicts can hurt an organization's, department or any business performance when they are not resolved.

"Mankind must evolve
for all human conflict
a method which rejects
revenge, aggression, and
retaliation. The foundation
of such a method is love."

– MARTIN LUTHER KING, JR.

The essential key to solving disagreements is to ask, "How can I honor, glorify and please Christ as Lord in this situation?" Many co-workers don't really understand when there in conflicts, someone will be wounded and get hurt emotionally. That is why it is so important that managers get involved as early as possible and attempt to diffuse and resolve any disputes or conflicts among the two parties in the workplace.

- Bring both parties together in a private place to discuss the issues.

- Lay down ground rules and allow each party to state their opinion.

- Let each party know this is a place of business and there will be no more interruption.

There are many problems and challenges that address our workplace today, and they transcend all kinds of businesses, governments, organizations, community affiliations and even churches. The enemy called the devil is working harder than ever against those in the workplace. The Bible says...*your adversary, the devil, as a roaring lion, walketh about, seeking whom he may devour* (1 Peter 5:8).

The workplace sometimes can be a battle of bad attitudes and conflicts that brings about hatred and bitterness and refusal to speak to one another. Workplace disputes are generally handled by avoiding the conflict, hoping it will go away; or through indirect means such as griping to your friends or colleagues about it, complaining to your supervisor, or complaining to the other person's supervisor. Following are principles that will help you address the problem you have with the person directly.

Here are some basic principles to help you deal
with disputes and conflicts in workplace:

- Understand there will be conflicts and disputes: We have to realize people are human, and they don't think the same, many times various disagreements, misunderstandings, and distinctions with various views of morals and values stands with one another that will show up in our relationships on the job.

- Communication is a way to solve conflicts: Many people are confounded with disputes and conflicts by ignoring the problems, which will not solve them. This will only cause more unforgiving spirits, bitterness and hatred among co-workers. Most problems can be solved by just being straightforward and not isolating the existing problems. "Talk it out".

- Taking responsibility in any disputes or conflicts: When you see others that are indulging in conflicts of any kind, don't join them by any means. Show them that you are a team and your heart says is Jesus pleased when we are indulging in conflicts?

- Co-workers agreeing to disagree without causing disunity: True wisdom and the leading of the Spirit of God always solved any conflicts or disputes. We, as mature employers and employees, need to understand we might not always see "eye to eye" in any every situation. This is not an excuse to allow pettiness to hinder our unity as a team.

- Dealing with difficult people: There are so many negative and lazy people on the job, who sometimes make you mad and frustrated. A lot of people are unreasonable, and they want things done their way only. We will run into people who will just not get it; they will not listen, deal, resolve, or handle things God's way.

There are many kinds of disputes that can be resolved, but it will take everyone to get involved. Management, employees, owners, CEOs and presidents cannot be exempt from participating in bringing about unity in the workplace. In the workplace, you must use diplomacy in dealing with others without causing bad feelings. Conflicts and disputes are inevitable in the workplace. No place of business is immune. When co-workers learn, equip and understand how to manage conflict, it can sometimes serve as a catalyst for change and an opportunity for spiritual and relational growth.

In the workplace is where co-workers will experience problems with one another, and attempts should always be made to solve the problems or conflicts that are confronted by employees. That's why disputes and conflicts must be viewed from a biblical view point. Once those in the workforce understand how to follow biblical guidelines, it will help eradicate conflicts and disputes. As employers and employees, we must have the attitude of reconciliation, forgiveness, loving one another and even loving our enemies. These are the values those in the workplace should reflect in dealing with one another when we offend one another.

*"Stay focused instead
of getting offended or
off track by others."*

– John Maxwell

WHERE DO CONFLICTS COME FROM?

Conflicts arise from a clash of perceptions, goals, or values in an arena where people care about the outcome. The breeding ground for conflict within the workplace lies in confusion or disagreement. Conflicts are fueled by internal negative communication that brings about havoc among co-workers. The lack of open communication drives conflict underground and can create a downward spiral of misunderstanding and hostility among co-workers.

Our ability to accomplish our goals and objectives depends on the cooperation and assistance from other stakeholders involved, which increases the opportunity for conflict. No one person can do the job without the input of someone else. When the other person is always late, has different priorities, misunderstands directions, or is playing office politics, then conflicts are created.

Sometimes, style differences also commonly happen at work. We all know that people do things in a different manner, thus, this might affect the work of others, and this, for sure, will cause conflicts among the employees. We all have our own style, designs, and distinct creative talents, thus, one idea may vary from another. However, in order to avoid any conflicts in the workplace, there must be an open communication and understanding in everything that should be done, and it must be agreed upon by each co-worker. Here is a list of where conflicts begin:

The "I am Always Right!" attitude: This type of attitude displays a lack of respect and tolerance for the views of others. Some people refuse to acknowledge that there are many ways to get the job done and think that there is only one way.

Resource Sharing: With limited resources, a conflict may arise due to the unequal sharing of resources.

Priorities: In a workplace, the priorities of people are linked to each other's work as they work in a team. Sometimes, wrong priorities will mess up the flow and may lead to conflict.

Misunderstandings: This is the source of most of the conflicts in life and in the workplace.

Power Struggles: The age-old "struggle for power" syndrome will lead to conflict most of the time in the workplace.

Values: This is a more deep-rooted problem which arises due to conflicting values. When people with conflicting sets of values come together, conflicts are inevitable.

Some people love to see conflict in the workplace, because they get their thrills over drama. In the workplace, you must deal with conflict and not run from it. It is natural to try to escape from the situation or to attack the other party. An escape response will only postpone a proper solution to a problem. Many people in the workplace fail to deal with the issues and conflicts at hand because of certain people's positions or naturally evil attitudes, so they allow them to do as they please, which should not be the case.

Most of the conflicts, which co-workers will face, can be resolved by just reaching out to the other person and communicating with them. Make them feel that they are part of the team no matter what their attitude is like. There will never be a perfect workplace with perfect employees, as we do not live in a perfect world!

CONFRONTATION AND RETALIATION WITHIN THE WORKPLACE

The biggest factor in marriages, friendships, among relatives, even in the workplace is unresolved conflicts. Many times, people refuse to confront issues they are facing. Effective communication is the foundation of all human endeavors; therefore, you must be diligent to keep the door

— 136 —

of communication open even in the face of conflict. The Apostle Paul cautioned us to *Make every effort to keep the unity of the Spirit through the bond of peace* (Ephesians 4:3 NIV). He also admonished *If it is possible, as much as it depends on you, live peaceably with all men* (Romans 12:18).

Confrontation is godly and is commanded. Retaliation is ungodly, and this is a forbidden attitude because it has to do with a dispute with a fellow member in the congregation. Confrontation can be positive or negative; a confrontation of any kind can be a little uncomfortable. Disputes can hinder your witness to the world (John 13:34).

When you refuse to deal with unresolved conflicts and disagreements by ignoring them because of the person's body language or because of fear of what they will say or do, you will hurt yourself or your workplace.

To confront a person generally means that one person is in disagreement with someone else's mannerisms, behavior, actions, etc. To confront someone can either be a positive or negative experience.

Confrontation and strife make the work environment an unhappy place for everyone. Difficult employees can turn a workplace upside down, slowing your company's production and ultimately impeding your success. Employees may be difficult because of past emotional and physical abuse, divorce, drug use, mental or just have a lonely meaningless life. If an employee is creating a disturbance in your workplace, you need to know how to quickly defuse the situation. The Lord wants us to confront rather than get revenge at someone. The disciples wanted to retaliate (Luke 6:29), but retaliation is to return the punishment. An offense is Satan's trap to deprive you of pleasing God and developing a productive relationship. When offense comes, someone must be prepared to take action to close the door to the situation. I strongly believe, according to the Word of God, that this is done through effective communication.

*"A man will be imprisoned
in a room with a door
that's locked as long as he
holds on to the past."*

DIVERSITY IN THE WORKPLACE

In the workplace today, there are a variety of differences between people in an organization. That sounds simple, but diversity encompasses race, gender, ethnic group, age, personality, cognitive style, tenure, organizational function, education, background and more. So why do many people think when it comes to diversity, they think first of ethnicity and race, and then gender? Diversity is much broader. Diversity is otherness or those human qualities that are different from our own and outside the groups, to which we belong, yet present in other individuals and groups. It's important to understand how these dimensions affect performance, motivation, success, and interactions with others.

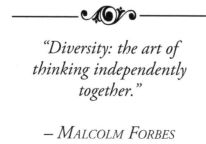

*"Diversity: the art of
thinking independently
together."*

– MALCOLM FORBES

Diversity not only involves how people perceive themselves, but how they perceive others. When people in general recognize and understand God didn't create everyone the same. We have to except our social and cultural diversities and learn how to deal with our cultural misunderstanding which is a big issue in our world today. In our daily lives, we all have to deal with people of difference, similar nature, and difference background. We will come daily into contact with people and co-worker who will have difference opinion and they will not see situation the same as you may see. Don't get mad and upset because they don't see eye to eye what you believe. Our customers and our co-workers we need to recognize and accept their right to their own beliefs and customs and, where practical, to make allowances for their differences and disabilities if we are to interact harmoniously with them.

"Workplace diversity is the key to survival and growth. I feel that people really want to contribute to the long-term success of their organizations and leaders should create a culture where everyone's perspective is heard."

-UNKNOWN

We must learn to accept difference, cultural, change, and difference that take place in the workplace. It will improve performance and customer service through a broadened base of knowledge and experience. A culturally diverse workforce is creative and flexible. It exposes customers and colleagues to new ideas, different ways of working and reaching decisions. Learning from customers and colleagues from other backgrounds, also broadens our own personal horizons and expands our own knowledge base, making us more efficient and tolerant as individuals.

When employees come from diverse backgrounds, they bring individual talents and experiences with them. This invariably contributes to an organization's overall growth. Embracing employees with different skills and cultural viewpoints helps in understanding the need of diversity. When you look on global scale diversity in the workplace leads to a variety of viewpoints and business ideas. This helps an organization to formulate the best business strategy, with its large pool of different ideas and solutions.

PREJUDICE IN THE WORKPLACE

Our world today is faced with so much prejudice and discrimination in our society and in the workplace. Prejudice can come in any form. It can be racial or social. Prejudice and discrimination in the workplace occurs when an employer does something or does not do something for an employee based upon prejudicial beliefs. Prejudicial actions can include: not hiring or firing someone, limiting benefits and perks, not hiring the handicapped, not promoting certain employees, sexual harassment, verbal abuse, a lower pay scale, and not giving a raise.

Discrimination can take place based on race, age, sexual orientation, disability, national origin, religion, or gender.

Discrimination in the workplace has come a long way in recent decades. It has learned to conceal itself even from those who make it happen. But it's there, despite decades of activism, legislation, and human resource programs to counter it and to promote an appreciation of diversity.

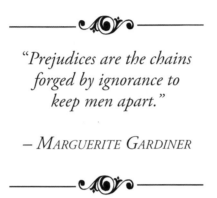

"Prejudices are the chains forged by ignorance to keep men apart."

— *MARGUERITE GARDINER*

Prejudice is a very old negative attitude. Prejudice is when a person makes a judgment, or has a preconceived idea, or an opinion, before the facts are known. There is really no room for discrimination in the workplace, whether the bias is racial, social, economic, religious, or intellectual. The root of all prejudice and violence in the workplace is bullying. Bullying underscores all forms of workplace prejudice, abuse, harassment, discrimination, and violence. The workplace bully is covertly and deeply prejudiced. There is some much politics in the work place that is very unprofessional. On many occasions, a workplace may be the source of so much conflict as in certain jobs it is who you know that helps you to get ahead. This has caused so must prejudice, hated and disrespect among co-workers and managers in workplace.

*"Education is important
because, first of all,
people need to know
that discrimination still
exists. It is still real in the
workplace, and we should
not take that for granted."*

— Alexis Herman

Prejudice is a destroyer of truth when our responses and attitudes are formed from a source of anything less than absolute truth among employees. Prejudice lies deeply hidden in our personalities. It prevents true communication, because it involves presumption based on an opinion or decision of mind formed without due examination of the facts or arguments. Due examination is necessary to achieve a just and impartial determination of someone or something without pre-judging. Prejudice and bigotry has divided our nation, our families, and our co-workers, because of race, creed, color, or faith. Prejudice and discrimination are negative manifestations of integrative power. We, as co-workers, must treat each other as team members. Here are a few things we must take in account to help stop prejudice and discrimination in the workplace:

- Stop pre-judging people.
- Treat people the way you want to be treated.
- Stand up for people who are being treated with prejudice.

Prejudice is very much like cancer or an epidemic that is passed on from generation to generation. That is why you must have a positive attitude that will help fight off the enemy of hatred, prejudice, conflict, and division in the workplace. Prejudice and discrimination must not be tolerated. Every employer should develop a strict code of ethics and conduct that is posted clearly and explained to every employee. Rules of acceptable conduct should be explicitly written and enforced. For the organization to be effective, you have to encourage feedback, innovation, and creativity so that the employees feel genuinely engaged. We need to create an environment of integrity, trust, and respect in this country that why we must banish prejudice for once and for all.

"I have a dream that my four little children will one day live in a nation where they will not be judged by the color of their skin, but by the content of their character."

— MARTIN LUTHER KING, JR.

THREATS IN WORKPLACE

In the workplace, today threats range from verbal abuse to physical violence. Threats in the workplace can be considered any type of intimidating behavior; however, the most common types of workplace threats are direct verbal threats, physical violence, sexual harassment, verbal attacks, such as name calling and profanity, obscene gestures and threat with imminent danger. Additionally, threats are also considered any actions that disrupt the peace of mind and safety of an individual and make people feel scared. Many people will use verbal threats to co-workers and tell them if you don't produce the product we need we will call your managers. There are many hurting people in the workplace, people who say things degrading to people that causes wounds and scars in their life that why you can't talk to people with any kinds of negative sharp attitude. This is not a professional attitude individual we must at all times we must communicate and work as a team.

In order to stop the threats or violent behavior within the workplace, an employer must provide essential security. The management has to react on three levels: duty to care, duty to warn, and the duty to act. Here are the four categories of threats that exist in workplace.

A direct threat: the targeted persons/places are known

An indirect threat: a violent act could occur

A veiled threat: depending how the threat is received

A conditional threat: if you do not do this, then...

It is essential for employees of any workplace to feel comfortable and safe in their environments in order to be productive and enjoy their jobs. Workplace intimidation and threats is a serious concern that can take many forms: verbal threats and critical remarks, sexual harassment, sabotage of a person's work or supplies, and even physical

"We've got a tragic history when it comes to race in this country. We've got a lot of pent-up anger and bitterness and misunderstanding. This country wants to move beyond these kinds of things."

— *Barack Obama*

"People who issue out threats are those who life is confused"

— *Bishop O.C. Isom, II*

violence. In order to stop workplace intimidation, individuals must not be afraid of threats of any person no matter of their title or position. When any form of threats is made to you seek the help of managers and law enforcement.

TRAINING IN THE WORKPLACE

Training is a necessity in the workplace. Without it, employees don't have a firm grasp on their responsibilities or duties. A company that lacks a proper training program cannot sustain a working business model, because the workplace is likely full of workers who have only a slight idea of how to complete their work. When a company does not properly train employees, they often have difficulty adapting to and understanding the workplace around them. While they may be able to complete their daily tasks, their performance usually lacks when compared to the more seasoned employees. Workers who aren't properly trained may become frustrated at their inability to perform at a high level, leading them to look elsewhere for a job or simply settle for mediocre performance.

With the growing competition among businesses in every industry, a lack of training in the employees can make the difference between maintaining success, and ultimate failure. Furthermore, without providing proper training among workers at the lower levels of the company, it is becoming increasingly challenging to find competent people to promote or hire for positions higher up in the corporate hierarchy.

God has a master plan for reaching and transforming a lost world. Jesus came with the purpose of reclaiming the world with the Gospel. His plan is simple and profound – taking twelve ordinary men, give them three years of training through association with Him, observing and obeying and send them out equipped with the Word, prayer and the Holy Spirit to reproduce disciples. That is the Lord's program, and it is reaching the world.

A wise trainer models with skills while teaching and maintaining a balance between classroom instruction and mentoring on the job.

Be imitators of me as I am of Christ (1 Corinthians 11:1). Our best teaching is often done on the job outside of any classroom. Jesus and His apostles apprenticed new leaders, combining verbal instruction with field work. Jesus taught the crowds by monologue, but he prepared novice leaders, by walking and chatting with them (Matthew 5:1-2). When Paul taught the Ephesian congregation, as reported in Acts 20:7, he did so discussing questions with them, not with a sermon. (The verb in the original Greek is "dialegomai", to discuss, discourse with, converse with, or discuss a question with another. The context of Acts 20:7 seems cordial and passionate, not a place and time for philosophical monologue, harangue or pulpit oratory.)

Each time you employ an employee for your small business, you must train him; the scope of training varies by employee and position. The success of your business depends on how well your employees perform and how your customers relate to them. Lack of employee training spells trouble for any company because it unfavorably impacts the company, internally and externally.

When a company offers education to its employees, it expects them to perform at optimum level after it's completed. While developing a training program, consider longevity, relevance, payment options, specificity and location. Even if training is given onsite by an existing employee, you must delegate her tasks to another employee while training is being conducted - this requires thoughtful decision-making. Training can be used to teach employees both subject-matter knowledge and information about the company's culture so they know how the company operates and what's expected of them.

Because training teaches new employees how to meet company expectations and gives existing employees a platform for improving current knowledge, it can provide the company a sense of stability. In the absence of training, employees become unsure of what's expected of them and may end up doing their work tasks inefficiently. Misunderstandings may ensue because employees aren't clear about the requirements. With confusion comes frustration, as employees become increasingly uncertain about their role in the company. And with frustration comes conflict, as employees can argue with each other or defy management because of improper training.

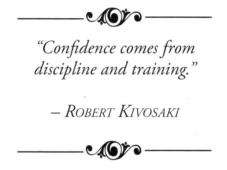

"Confidence comes from discipline and training."

— ROBERT KIVOSAKI

As employees leave, you must replace them. Too many departures reflect negatively on the company and indicate the inability to retain workers. Further, each time someone leaves, it puts you back at square one. If the root of the problem, which is lack of training, is not fixed, the cycle keeps repeating itself. High turnover costs the company money. Each time an employee is terminated, you must spend money to hire someone else. This includes the time and money spent processing termination paperwork, advertising for someone new, interviewing job applicants, processing new-hire paperwork, and allowing existing employees and the new worker time to adjust to each other. If these adjustments happen too frequently, existing employees may grow tired of it.

A well-trained and committed employee is likely to remain with the company. Because you took the time to ensure that she receives proper training, she's more motivated to give back to the company. An employee who lacks proper training is unmotivated because she lacks the knowledge needed to serve your customers. This results in low productivity and inaccurate work, which hurts the company's bottom line.

When training and development result in better outcomes, employees tend to display a greater sense of ownership and pride in their work. This can help lead to increased productivity and efficiency, and of course, an increase in job satisfaction. Staff who are happy in their work are more likely to work harder and be more valuable to the company, which will in turn, put the company in a stronger position.

WORKPLACE DRAMA

From my personal experience in the workplace, I have learned where there are human relationships, there is potential for drama to occur. We as human beings create a lot of drama when we don't know how to master our energy or clear the fog to see the bigger picture." Every workplace has a queen or king drama person who love Dealing with drama in the workplace. Drama has the potential to suck the life out of you, and to kill your motivation, and for many of co-workers, it leaves them thinking: "I hate my job". Drama in the workplace causes many problems and too many hurt feelings when co-workers hate each other. Every workplace has all kinds of drama stoppers. This kind of attitude just

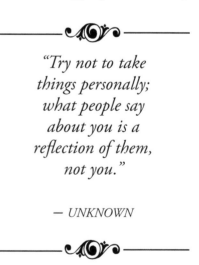

"Try not to take things personally; what people say about you is a reflection of them, not you."

— *UNKNOWN*

makes people mad and upset then before you know it; it distracts them from what is really important working as a team.

Life is too short for employers or employees to waste time been angry or frustrated over small trivial matter in the workplace. That why we must keep the drama down in workplace with that said, we must be careful not to criticize our co-workers for having a different view and outlook on things that you do. We must avoid being critical using negative words towards others that will hurt them and cause must pain in their life. Your choice of words when interacting with co-workers, managers, and customers is vital. When you speak critical or negative words, the effect can be long lasting. Positive words and interactions, instead, increase workplace happiness and productivity. Before you speak, ask yourself whether your listener will hear you diminish or "make smaller" the person who is the focus of the conversation. In other words, will your listener think less respectfully about the person? If so, then seriously consider remaining silent. Communicating about issues directly with those involved is better than to speak about others behind their backs.

There are moments in everyone's life in the workplace we become dramatic because we don't get our way. However, there are also people that view all of life's changes as an opportunity to react in an overly dramatic fashion. So, simply refuse to be pulled in. She will undoubtedly try to reel you in with stories, tears, outbursts or even arguments, basically anything that will direct attention to her. So, regardless of what she does retain your cool and let it pass over you. Show her and everyone else around that you are the bigger person by retaining your poise in spite of her meltdowns. So here are some ways to diffuse people who love to stir up drama in workplace.

*"The drama of life always
begins with those people who
are emotional disturbed."*

Point out to her/him that they are making a scene. Most of the time, a drama queen or king might be creating a scene unknowingly and this would by no means escape their senses. However, very rarely does anyone have the guts required to tell them directly that they are causing a scene, and could they please tone their behavior down a little. Now, that being said at this point those who love to keep up drama may launch a full frontal attack on you letting you know that a scene is appropriate, but once again retain your cool and let them know this is not the correct time or place but that you would be glad to discuss it with them at a later, more private time.

If all else fails, walk away. The entire point of being a drama king and queen is to gain attention. By walking away completely, you are refusing to let them accomplish the entire objective of their dramatic behavior. Just ignore them that will diffuse all of their attention and make them see it don't work anymore.

When dealing with true drama kings and queens in the workplace, the results can be stressful to the breaking point. So, at some point, especially for those of us dealing with those who love to keep up drama on a daily basis, it is imperative to learn how to diffuse their dramatic behavior without looking like an unsympathetic or uncaring person yourself. But rest assured, with my tips you will not only be able to diffuse their dramatic behavior, but you will walk away looking like the only rose in a field of thistles. Negativity is the number one productivity problem in the workplace. Signs of negativity include backstabbing, gossiping, power struggles and lack of teamwork. The end result is absenteeism, low morale and turnover that leased to confusion.

No matter what you call it, disruptive behavior, low morale, insubordination, workplace bullying, or negativity: It's ALL DRAMA.

FEUDING IN WORKPLACE

In our world today, there is the negative attitude of feuding among Republicans and Democrats, appointed officials and organizations, and feuding in workplace among employees. Many times when their values seem to conflict and they can't get along with each other they begin to dislike one another. Feuds feed on everything. Even a simple rearrangement of offices, change, or people they just don't like will cause controversy that consumes everyone and stops all work in the workplace. There are many bullies in workplace that love to keep stirring up things between co-workers that always causes arguments, fall-outs, disagreements, strong languages of words are used which cause feuding in workplace. Bitter rivalries and cold shoulders are among many co-workers in the workplace. Many workplaces remind you of days of the Hatfield's & McCoy's with a small misunderstanding escalated resentment and into all-out warfare between the families.

Conflict will always arise in the workplace, and it will always bring about misunderstandings, dislike, division, hurt feeling, and disunity.

Whether you like it or not you are families in the workplace. You are there eight hours or more with each other, working, laughing, trying to solve problems, and sharing your feeling with each other as a team that is similar to a family. Here are some tips for resolving feuding in workplace.

Meet with the feuding co-workers to see if you can remedy the situation. Do this quickly to avoid letting it fester and spiral out of control in workplace.

Make known to your boss the situation so that they're not blindsided by any necessary disciplinary actions now or in the future.

Involve HR as necessary, which could be as an independent mediator, to put difficult employees on notice or probation, or to begin the process of transferring the troublemakers to another department or location.

Advocate an environment of respect, tolerance, and civility in the office.

Maintain an open dialogue with your employees. Freely sharing information and have meeting that will help with the problems with employees who love to keep feuding, gossip and rumors.

Review your policies on use of company email and social media sites. Some disgruntled employees will take their rants online either within or outside of the company. Know your company's electronic media policies and communicate them with all employees.

"I believe that everything happens for a reason. People change so that you can learn to let go, things go wrong so that you appreciate them when they're right, you believe lies so you eventually learn to trust no one but yourself, and sometimes good things fall apart so better things can fall together."

– MARILYN MONROE

Developing a strong team environment is an important factor in fostering cooperation and reducing negative interactions among employees. Encourage employees to think of their co-workers as internal customers waiting to be served. This will promote respectful communication and willingness helps each other. A sense of camaraderie helps build trust and empathy and may cause employees to modify negative behavior themselves, refuse to feud with each other, so they can work as a team.

CHANGE CAUSES RESISTANCE WHICH CAUSE CONFLICT IN WORKPLACE

Managing change in the workplace is a constant for all leaders. To remain relevant as a business you must regularly redefine your way of operating, your product/service offerings and the impact you have on your customers and broader community. For most people, any change is uncomfortable. Therefore, when managing change in the workplace, it is your job is to help people see that whatever they've been doing in the past can no longer take place. Managers and employees should bear in mind that change is inevitable, so neither they, nor the business, will be relevant without change. When many leaders bring to the table to their employees uttering the word "change" is equivalent of yelling shark in workplace.

One of the reasons may be that, many times, change places us squarely between "a rock and a hard place".

We know that change is necessary so we can't back away from it, but we also know it's going to be really hard for some people, and that a lot of difficult conversations probably lie ahead. Many people in workplace don't like change because change seems too uncomfortable. It means a departure from what is familiar and comfortable, to embrace that which is unknown and risky. Yet, because the human condition resists change so dramatically, many business keep looking for ways to perfect what they are doing, so they may attract other customers and keep us with time. Effectively managing the workplace means not fearing or resisting change and challenges, by empowering management and employees with the necessary skills to effectively manage life changes. Strategically preparing managers and employees catalyzes better organizational performance – regardless what changes you might face.

Here is a beautiful and poetic exposition of the different seasons we are expecting to see: *For everything there is a season. A time to keep and a time to cast away* (Ecclesiastes 3:1-8). Now the application of this verse is that people must expect change in workplace; it's simply inevitable.

Nothing continues unchanged or it will die, or the people become bored. We continue to change our product, service, and ways of doing things, like technology and styles, but when it comes to the things within our workplace, many people refuse to change. No business or organization can escape change.

So many people in workplace get used to what they are doing, and they find that what they are already doing to be somewhat meaningful and comfortable for them. When employees don't find change in workforce to be meaningful, then the assumption is that the problem is not with the people but rather with their administration.

Workforces are comprised of people — and most people don't like to change. "Change" is an emotionally packed word. For some, it is invigorating and exciting. For others, it is terrifying and threatening. Most people's lives are based on routines — doing the same things the same way, day after day.

Their unspoken and often unconscious expectation is that everything will stay the same. As soon as you interrupt their routine, they resist. An individual's reaction to change is complex but certainly involves personality, temperament, giftedness, and life experiences. Changing your attitude will, in turn, change your results. While others are still moaning and groaning, you'll be on the phone with future customers, discussing your new opportunity.

Your energy and new improved attitude will become contagious and will spread quickly throughout your company. You will be a positive influence to those around you. It is all up to you.

So the next time you are presented with a change, remember to stay positive and to challenge yourself to find the opportunity within it. Your choice to stay positive is all in your mind. You control your mind; you control the situation; you control the outcome and the destiny of your company.

HOW TO SOLVE CONFLICT IN THE WORKPLACE

There are many areas within the workplace where conflict will develop. However it is caused, it leads to conflict and this may be due to negative co-workers and bad leadership. Everyone knows what conflict is and why it is so harmful. Some co-workers blame, argue, or gossip because they have a mean-spirited attitude, while others quietly push buttons, offer subtle digs, passively infuriate, or adopt a cool, collected demeanor. It is important that co-workers should not have an evil attitude. They must avoid them at all cost. Team unity, first and foremost, is about trust — the willingness to be vulnerable with your teammates and to be heard and supported by them in return.

"Change will not come if we wait for some other person or some other time. We are the ones we've been waiting for. We are the change that we seek."

— BARACK OBAMA

Conflict at the place of work is centered on quarreling, because someone wants recognition, honor, power, glory, and pleasure. To have a healthy workplace, a team needs diversity. People who bring a lot of different skills, knowledge, experiences, values, attitudes, and viewpoints to the table can often achieve far more than a group with very similar backgrounds. Having a diversity of opinions and viewpoints on a team can be one of its greatest strengths posed in an organization. However, it is this very diversity that creates problems in teams.

When you work with others, it is inevitable that the occasional conflict in the workplace will arise. We all have our own points of view, ways of viewing a situation, ways of wanting to be communicated with, ways of being led and managed, ways of resolving problems, and given the right circumstances, these differences of opinion can escalate into a full-blown conflict in the workplace. How you decide to handle conflicts which may come up will determine whether those conflicts will end up strengthening the team as a whole or collapse it. Before stepping in to help in any conflict resolution effort, it is critical to understand that you cannot ignore aspects such as:

Emotions — they will likely be running high.

People — have different perspectives on what has happened, or what caused the conflict in the workplace.

Perceptions — each party will believe that their perspective is right.

Conflict in the workplace can be a positive thing, provided it is managed and dealt with promptly. A signature tune of any high-performance team is that the team members are open to hearing other points of view and learning from them rather than allowing them to escalate into bitter disputes within the team. The ability to deal with conflict as it emerges will allow the workplace to stay healthy and vibrant. Team members learn conflict resolution skills through both the careful guidance of one another by their team leader and by being trained in the skills that enable them to communicate, interact, negotiate, and provide feedback effectively. Unfortunately, many organizations don't see the value in spending money to train their employees in these so called 'soft' skills.

This is one of the reasons why many organizations don't score high on performance — they underestimate the value and the impact of the social system within their organization — thereby condemning themselves to a performance that is less effective and powerful than it could be. Hopefully, this doesn't happen in your place of business — and that conflict in your workplace is easily handled.

"You need to be aware of what others are doing, applaud their efforts, acknowledge their successes, and encourage them in their pursuits. When we all help one another, everybody wins."

–JIM STOVALL

THE EFFECTS OF DISHARMONY IN THE WORKPLACE

Managers spend one-third of their workday attending to conflict in the workplace. Conflict is also responsible for the majority of work performance problems. The difference between a happy workplace and a workplace on edge with backbiting, gossip, and conflict can be the difference between a productive and successful business.

Many people in the workforce have suffered from the effects of gossip, poor communication, and conflict. Many co-workers have experienced selfish behaviors that come from bad attitudes causing frustration and confusion. When you work with extremely difficult people, they have the capacity to debilitate Individuals, teams, and even whole organizations, hence the need to learn how to be patient and to harmonize.

Even when a person on the job has a great attitude, incompetence can be a huge distraction to other people in the organization, because they have to spend a lot of extra time trying to help someone become competent. Negative attitudes and conflicts in the workplace are issues that exist in the workforce today. When there is poor communication and conflict among co-workers, it only creates a path of destruction in an organization.

This will only bring about toxic behavior that will prevent the growth of the environment of the workplace. Before any organization can solve a problem, they have to be educated and fully understand the situation at hand. There are those in the workplace who bring about chaos and conflict, which causes frustration, discouragement, and confusion. When a person's attitude changes in the workplace, it can substitute for personal growth. So it is very important that every co-worker must evaluate their attitude toward one another others.

"Attitude is a little thing that makes a big difference."

—WINSTON CHURCHILL

THE PROPER ATTITUDE WE SHOULD BRING TO WORK TO CREATE A TEAM ENVIRONMENT

Whether you consider yourself to have a good or bad attitude, your attitude and emotions will bring a certain environment in workplace.

- You should always have a smile on your face and speak.
- You should bring your heart to work each day and leave your drama at home.
- You should always interact as a team and support each other to reach your goal each day.
- You should develop a healthy relationship.
- You should make sure you follow through with your customers.
- You should always listen to your customer.
- You should always communicate positive and skillful.
- You should understand a team is a family more than collogues.

The attitudes of employees in the workplace can have a significant effect on the business as a whole. Attitude is one of the hidden, hard-to-measure factors that end up being crucial to the success of a company. Whether for better or for worse, employee attitudes tend to have a drastic impact on the productivity of a business, both directly and through the effect on other job-related factors. When there is a dismantle team in the workplace, it will increase stress and cripple productivity.

Attitude is so important in the work environment. Positive attitudes can affect productivity and enhance the working relationships between colleagues. If you want to work in an environment where there are motivated and empowered employees, then individuals need to maintain positive healthy attitudes. Employers and employees must be willing to enforce positive attitudes. Negativity is destructive and can cause an organization to fail to meet its goals.

"The only disability in life is a bad attitude."

-SCOTT HAMILTON

ABOUT THE AUTHOR

O. C. Isom, II is the founder and Senior Pastor of Word up Apostolic Ministries. He has a lovely wife Marilyn, two daughters, Tiffany and Karissa, and a son Andre. He is the Bishop of the State of Michigan of the International Circle of Faith. He works at Lakeland Regional Medical Center, St. Joseph, Michigan. He has a Bachelor's Degree in Theology and a Master's Degree in Counseling from Cypress Bible College in Van, Texas. He is the author of *Wounds Caused by Gossip* and Wounds Caused by Gossip Ministry. He has over forty years of experience in the workplace dealing with conflicts and attitudes that have hurt many people, emotionally and mentally. For many years, he has sought to find a beautiful groundbreaking solution that will restore pride and bring about restoration and results back into workplace. He has written this book which covers the complete spectrum in the workplace. He began his focus on educating leaders and co-workers on how to improve communication skills in all areas at places of work. Our personal beliefs, prejudices, ideals, and attitudes direct our behavior and our judgment regarding the behavior of others, with others' defenses against uncertainly being much more obvious to us than our own. That is why we must create a relationship environment in the workplace that is more honest, open, respectful, and effective, which will cause your organization to grow.

"Any conflict can be resolved. The solution is you have to communicate."

– O. C. Isom, II

THE POWER OF PRAYER IN THE WORKPLACE

In the Name of Jesus Christ, which is the final authority. As we start this blessed day as your servant, I thank you for blessing me with the skills and abilities to be a blessing on my job. Lord, I ask you for your grace and mercy because upon me when I'm faced with gossip, negative attitudes and conflicts give me the strength to ignore sinful ways of the enemy. Jesus allows me to speak well to my co-workers, customers with a positive attitude and cause me to display a Christian lifestyle. I ask your blessing over all I say, think, decide, and do today. Jesus I realize I will be hurt, wounded, stress and abused in workplace, but when I'm confused, guide me and strengthen me by your empowerment and give me the grace to forgive those who have spitefully mistreated and hurt me. Jesus, I realize I have to love mine enemies and don't use revenge against them because you promise to fight my battles. Allow your protection and guardian angels to keep you from all harm as you trust in God's Word.

For he shall give his angels charge over thee, to
keep thee in all thy ways (Psalms 91:11).

Bless my creativity, my ideas, and my energy so that everything I do may bring joy and a smile to all I come in contact with. Bless every employee on job that we may work as a team that we may glorified God in all we do! In the precious name of Jesus, I pray. Amen!

Be careful for nothing; but in everything by prayer and supplication with thanksgiving let your requests be made known unto God (Philippians 4:6).

ABOUT WOUNDS CAUSED BY GOSSIP MINISTRY

Wounds Caused by Gossip Ministry has been empowered by kingdom of God to equips, train, inform, educate, that we may bring the body of Christ together as one in the spirit. It is time for the church of the living God to help restore our workplace, churches, families, and communities back to God. We live in a society that is flooded with gossip and conflicts. And we just ignore it, our evening news, magazines, inquiry; many people enjoy gossip and conflicts. But what happen when gossip and conflict infiltrate the workplace and the church. We must realize the core of our problems that we are faced with today is gossip and conflicts that has effect many and cause them to be wounded. Many people can endure all kinds of physical affliction, but when our spirit is wounded and a wounded-spirited person is someone who has been hurt and bruised and/or damaged in their spirit – it can be very painful and hurtful. A wounded spirit comes as a result of a re-action to negative words, events, actions, or a violation of your person or rights – a re-action that crushes you, knocks you down and from which you cannot seem to rise. It crushes an area of your life – your spirit – which is quite devastating in how it affects us. It seems we cannot heal ourselves of a wounded spirit.

We see our churches, workplace and even our political government have failed. When we as believers who believe in the power of God's Word, we can put a stop to gossip and conflicts in our world today and brings about kingdom changes. We as a people must bring God back in our lives, workplace and our churches and align ourselves under the might hands of God. That why this ministry called Wounds Caused by Gossip Ministry has been orchestrate by God to impact and to transform attitudes that don't line up with the Word of God.

It is time for us as a people to achieve our spiritual and natural goals by changing our environment in our workplace and our churches so we can see His will done in our lives as it is in heaven. Many people individual love this ministry. Many of them have given their testimony how your books on gossip and conflict has cause me to change and be deliver from emotional wounds. In order for us to change we as leaders in workplace and those in the church must understand what is the problem that is hurting and eating away in the workplace and the church? When we understand that gossip and conflict is the basis problems we them must embrace these evil attitudes and find biblical answers to help us overcome these attitudes. Leaders must begin using strategy such as seminars, workshops, and resources that will address issues of gossip and conflicts.

*"We must shine the light
of God's Word and expose
gossip and conflicts."*

MINISTRY INFORMATION AND RESOURCES

You can contact the author or purchase other material and products through:

WORD UP APOSTOLIC MINISTRIES

P.O. BOX 8244

BENTON HARBOR, MI, 49023

269-519-0459 or 269-252-9510

Fax: 269-927-3618

Services Times

9:30 a.m. - Morning Manna

11:30 a.m. - Worship Service

6:00 p.m. - Prayer/Deliverance

6:00 p.m. - Bible Study

DID YOU ENJOY THIS BOOK?

Bishop Isom would love to hear from you! Please let him know if this book has enlightened or educated you or has touched your heart in one way or the other and if at all has made you have a change of heart regarding having a positive attitude in workplace.

Rickyisom628@yahoo.com

www.wordupchurch.org

"Every employer and employee bring one thing to work every day and that is attitude." O.C. Isom, II

BIBLIOGRAPHY

Neeta, Sharma. Communication at Work. The *ability* to communicate is the heart of any business, is the most important of all entrepreneurial *skills*. 2010

Kristina L. Guo, PhD and Yesenia Sanchez, MPH. Workplace Communication. Fundamental of communication is a means of transmitting information and making oneself understood by another or others. 2005

Miranda Brookins, Demand Media. Reasons for Poor Communication in the Workplace. Even though communication is recognized as a key to a successful work environment, companies often struggle with *poor communication* in their *workplaces*. 2014

Susan M. Heathfield. How to Manage Gossip at Work. Gossip is rampant in most workplaces. Sometimes, it seems as if people have nothing better to do than gossip about each other. 2014

Lalla Scotter, Demand Media. How to Deal with Tattletale Co-workers. In workplaces throughout the world, there are all kinds of toxic people making their co-workers' lives miserable. One of the worst types is the office tattletale.2014

Susan M. Heathfield. How to Tackle Annoying Employee Habits and Issues. Have you ever worked alongside an employee who had poor personal hygiene, foul smelling clothes or breath? 2014

Ronald G. Shapiro, Ph. D., Maluniu, Allie. How to Be a Leader in the Workplace. Effective leadership is an important skill in the professional arena. A skilled leader is a strong communicator, motivator and problem solver. 2014

Justin, Thompson. Cliques in the workplace: The good, the bad & the reality. I'm sure if you sat back and thought about all the people you work with, you could identify several *cliques* in your *workplace*. 2011

Nathan, Chandler. 10 Tips for Managing Conflict in the Workplace. Workplace conflict is an unavoidable consequence of professional life. 2014

Peacemaker Ministries. Resolving Everyday Conflicts: In Workplace. Understand the source and nature of conflict and how we react to conflict and how to react more constructively to conflict.

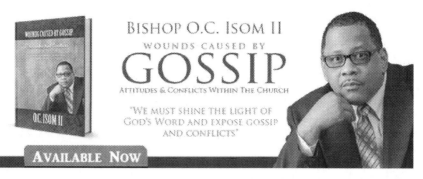
Wounds Caused by Gossip Attitudes and Conflicts in Church

In this timely and powerful new book, O.C. Isom II unveils the sinful attitudes of gossip which bring about conflicts church. For far too long this sinful epidemic has polluted the church and have caused division and emotional wounds in people lives. Wounds Caused by Gossip is a very serious book and a divine extinguisher that will expose gossip and conflicts in Church. You'll learn:

- Gossip is sinful and a tool of the Devil
- Conflicts, feuding and division in church
- Dealing with bitterness, unforgivness and emotional wounds
- Promoting a transforming kingdom mind-set.

With passion and clarity, O.C. Isom equips readers to move beyond carnal and negative attitudes. He is excited for Christian to live in victory over gossip and conflicts In Jesus Christ by embracing a transforming kingdom mind-set that will cause you to develop a relationship between one another. You can order this book at: Amazon, Barnes & Nobles, or email Rickyisom628@yahoo.com

No Souls Left Behind